The Invention of Heterosexual Culture

The Invention of Heterosexual Culture

Louis-Georges Tin

The MIT Press   Cambridge, Massachusetts   London, England

This work, published as part of a program providing publication assistance, received financial support from the French Ministry of Foreign Affairs, the Cultural Services of the French Embassy in the United States, and FACE (French American Cultural Exchange).

MIT Press books may be purchased at special quantity discounts for business or sales promotional use. For information, please email special_sales@mitpress.mit.edu or write to Special Sales Department, The MIT Press, 55 Hayward Street, Cambridge, MA 02142.

This book was set in Adobe Garamond and Univers Condensed by the MIT Press. Printed and bound in the United States of America.

Library of Congress Cataloging-in-Publication Data
Tin, Louis-Georges.
[Invention de la culture hétérosexuelle. English]
The invention of heterosexual culture / Louis-Georges Tin.
    p. cm.
Originally published by Editions Autrement in 2008 as: L'invention de la culture hétérosexuelle.
Includes bibliographical references and index.
ISBN 978-0-262-01770-1 (hbk. : alk. paper)
1. Heterosexuality—History. I. Title.
HQ23.T57 2012
306.76′4—dc23
2011051327

10 9 8 7 6 5 4 3 2 1

Contents

Preface

Paradoxically, the blossoming of gay and lesbian cultures suggests that it is now possible to review heterosexuality in a fresh light. Over the centuries, thousands of studies have explored issues of heterosexual love, sex, marriage, and the family, whereas heterosexuality itself rarely rates a mention. It is usually taken for granted as a self-evident point of departure—a viewpoint that is also a blind spot. Heterosexuality is assumed to be ever-present as a matter of course and has escaped analysis, as if it is transparent to itself. This absence of analysis is itself a striking if seldom acknowledged fact.

That said, the world at large appears obsessed by the imagery of the heterosexual couple. Fairy tales, novels, cinema and television, newspapers and magazines, advertising and pop music: all celebrate the pairing of man and woman. For most heterosexuals, at least, it is an invisible kingdom where heterosexuality reigns supreme and where everything in nature is in its place and hence natural. On this topic, the most basic—as well as the most radical—questions have not been resolved or even asked. Notably, in the first instance, is the question of causes. Why are certain individuals drawn primarily to members of the opposite sex? The question may seem absurd or even unnecessarily provocative, but it raises a point that is far from obvious to the extent that the root cause of this phenomenon remains largely unexplored.

Although, in general, heterosexuality may seem to be the most natural thing in the world, it is far from easy to justify it on purely biological terms. Few people ever ask themselves whether attraction to the opposite sex is triggered by a physiological mechanism. The question commonly asked by biologists and doctors—and, for that matter, by society as a whole—is what causes people to be drawn to persons of the same sex. Current research has been largely directed toward otherness and the heuristically abnormal. Homosexuality rather than heterosexuality has been explored and explained.

The facile justification for heterosexuality is that it is essential for the reproduction of the species. This explanation puts the end before the means in that no specific cause is identified (hormonal, neuronal, psychological?). Accordingly, heterosexuality has its origins in genetic necessity, or if that statement seems unduly laconic, it can be reformulated in more Darwinian terms: heterosexual behavior, irrespective of the factors underpinning it, represents the sole means of ensuring human reproduction and therefore is conducive to natural selection and the evolution of the species.

But this explanation is far from satisfactory. Above all, it fails to pinpoint the principle that underlies heterosexual behavior. Can it be sourced to the brain, the genes, the hormones, or somewhere else? Even supposing that one acknowledges the heterosexual imperative that is implicit in biological reproduction, it is more difficult to account for the essentially heterosexual structure of human society. After copulation, there is no apparent need for a couple to continue together, and most mammals part company rapidly thereafter. Even in the case of primates that often coexist in social groups, there is scant justification for concluding that some form of heterosexuality is fundamental to their social structure. Certainly, biological reproduction is heterosexual, but social structures are much more complex, based as they are on strictly observed patterns of dominance, rivalry, cooperation, and interaction. The heterosexual couple is seldom the basic component cell of the group and, in many instances, is not even necessary for the education of the young. It is clear that heterosexuality is not a dominant feature of animal societies. Some form of instinct is doubtlessly at work between the opposite sexes during ovulation, and this behavior is heterosexual. But in reality, to be precise, only humans have built societies on the basis of heterosexuality.

All human societies are not heterosexual. One need look no further than archaic or classical Greece as a famous but by no means isolated example among Indo-Europeans in general.[1] It is apparent that Greek society and others like it were heterosexual only with respect to biological procreation. This should not be taken to imply that Greek society was homosexual, inasmuch as pederastic initiation was a practice quite distinct from what we now mean by homosexuality. As recent studies[2] have demonstrated, however, the question of homosexual versus heterosexual orientation is scarcely relevant. Although the Greek male typically sought a female to ensure continuation of the family line, it is evident that heterosexuality itself was not the basis on which ancient Greek society was constructed.

To substantiate this argument, a comparison can be established with food. In all human societies, there are food-related practices, and they are indispensable to the survival of individuals. But all societies do not necessarily construct a culture of gastronomy as, for example, in France. The art of the table, of wine, and of cheeses, the rituals, the service, the conviviality, the cookbooks, the restaurant guides, the systems of classification and stars, the televised cooking shows are some of the elements that define French gastronomy. Other societies have developed food practices that are less diverse and less ritualized, and they are based primarily on the material necessities for survival. Granted, those attitudes are reflected in principles and codes, and they sometimes specify celebrations when food occupies a particular place. But they do not add up to what can truly be called a culture of gastronomy. In these numerous contexts and not only in ancient or far-flung societies like those of the Amazon or New Guinea, food is at the same time both necessary and secondary, and, nevertheless, it is not elevated to the rank of sacred and collective ritual. In short, eating is universal, whereas gastronomy is not.

At the same time, heterosexual practices are universal, whereas the culture of heterosexuality is not. Although human nature is manifestly heterosexual, which allows the reproduction of the species, human cultures are not necessarily heterosexual—that is, they do not always give symbolic primacy to the man-woman couple and to love in its cultural, literary, or artistic representations, as close study of ancient and archaic civilizations reveals.

Going further, we could ask whether heterosexual cultures—that is, those where attraction to the opposite sex predominates and is cultivated, and celebrated—are no more than a specific case that historical reasons related to economic expansion and colonization have apparently rendered general. Indeed, in many cultures where heterosexual practices are the norm, they are seldom associated with love and even less with passion. They derive from a sense of social obligation that regulates sexual relations (more often than not with the male as the dominant partner) so that male desire for a female is simultaneously regarded as necessary yet secondary. This goes some way toward explaining why such cultures have little place for love. The importance assigned to love—or more exactly, to heterosexual love—seems to be a peculiarity of Western societies, as American historian John Boswell has pointed out:

> Industrial society has made a veritable obsession of this subject. To an observer of the modern West's cultural monuments, it would probably seem that romantic love was the primary interest of industrial society in the nineteenth and twentieth centuries. An overwhelming proportion of popular literature, popular art, and popular music have as their central focus the seeking out, celebration of, or lament over romantic love, which is surprising and noteworthy considering that the vast majority of the population to which these cultural messages are directed is either already married or too young or old to be involved in such pursuits. Those immersed in this "sea of love"[3] tend to take it for granted; even many scholars of the subject fail to notice how remarkable is the degree of its prominence in the cultures in which they grew up. Very few premodern or nonindustrialized contemporary cultures would agree with the contention— uncontroversial in the West—that "the purpose of a man is to love a woman, and the purpose of a woman is to love a man."[4] Most human beings in most times and places would find this a very meager measure of human value.
>
> In other cultures and in premodern Western societies, other subjects have formed the primary material of public culture: celebration of heroic figures or events; reflections on the seasons; observations on the success, failure, or precariousness of agricultural cycles; histories of families (in which romantic love plays a small role, if any); explorations or elaborations of religious or political traditions.[5]

Although heterosexual procreation is the biological basis for human society, heterosexual culture is only one construct among many, and in this sense, it should not be presented as a unique or universal model. What this implies is a need to explore as never before when, how, and why our society began to celebrate the heterosexual couple. What is needed is an exploration of the origins of the sociosexual context in which we live today, a subject that has never been studied in these terms. But to accomplish this requires nothing less than an epistemological revolution, which means taking heterosexuality out of the "order of nature" and putting it within the "order of time"—that is, history.

PART I

Chivalric Opposition to Heterosexual Culture

To situate heterosexual culture in historical perspective, it is appropriate to establish when heterosexual culture made its first appearance in Western society. Toward the beginning of the twelfth century, it emerged in the West with what is often termed *courtly love*. In previous periods, the man-women couple had not been celebrated. Although it may have been acknowledged from time to time in specific contexts, it was never a concept deemed worthy of more than passing interest. As of the early twelfth century, however, heterosexuality began to emerge as a recurrent theme in art and literature. It merited protracted and enthusiastic scrutiny and analysis. It became endlessly analyzed, sung about, celebrated, and exalted. It became a cultural phenomenon—even a cult object.

The Middle Ages: From a Homosocial to a Heterosexual Culture

The courtly ethic that came to prominence in the West fostered the emergence of a culture based on man-woman relationships. All-male friendships—the very stuff of heroic legend—were increasingly suspect, widely criticized, and often maligned. This transition from a formerly homosocial world to a modern heterosexual culture merits detailed examination. The process of substitution was protracted, complex, and onerous, and there was considerable and diversified opposition to the new heterosexual culture. It is perhaps for this reason that the culture's emergence is nowhere more evident than in the resistance it engendered, most notably in the form of the chivalric tradition.

The Chivalric Tradition and the Celebration of Manly Love

Perhaps the most notable resistance came from warriors in particular and the nobility in general. Up to this point, feudal culture had been rooted in an exclusively male universe. Men—and above all, men of action—frequently lived in a world far removed from that of womankind. Men were trained to exhibit individual courage and integrity as loyal servants and vassals of a rigid feudal order. Serving as members of a group facing common challenges and dangers spawned a heightened sense of achievement and forged strong bonds that often went beyond those of simple camaraderie. Male friendships frequently lasted a lifetime[1] and were affirmed in the most fervent terms, betraying a mix of tenderness and military robustness difficult to conceive of today. These passionate male friendships intensified in the course of knightly involvement in adventure, conflict, and war and were often regarded as an essential part of the chivalric ideal. Their nature and symbolic content have been succinctly described by Georges Duby:

> Among the knights of the twelfth century—as within the Church—normal love, the love that caused one to forget oneself, to surpass oneself in mighty deeds for the glory of a friend, was homosexual. I do not mean that it necessarily led to physical complicity, but it was very obviously the love between men, strengthened by the values of loyalty and service drawn from vassalic morality, that was seen as the basis of order and peace, and it was to this that the moralists naturally transferred the new fervor with which the speculation of theologians had impregnated the word *amor*. When, on the other hand, men of the Church were concerned with the relations between men and women—and this was one of their chief preoccupations, since they were trying, at this period, to construct an ethic of marriage and strengthen the framework of the conjugal union, which was the only place, according to them, where licit heterosexual relations might take place—they were extremely cagey. This was because, in this case, sex necessarily intervened and because sex was sin, the stumbling block.[2]

Duby rightly stresses the importance of male *amor* in feudal society and points out that it was a culture where love between males was the norm, a homosexual love albeit not necessarily physically consummated. For present purposes and to preclude any misunderstanding, we favor the term *homosociality*.

This view of feudal society is shared by John Boswell, who has pointed out that the man-woman couple and the cult of heterosexual love are by no means universal in anthropological terms, inasmuch as "In other cultures and in premodern Western societies, other subjects have formed the primary material of public culture: celebration of heroic figures or events, among others."[3] The evidence suggests that the man-woman pairing was not regarded as a major priority of feudal society before the advent of courtly love. Heterosexuality was regarded as necessary but secondary; passions and enthusiasms were reserved for "celebration of heroic figures" (Boswell) and for "love between men, strengthened by the values of loyalty and service drawn from vassalic morality" (Duby).

History records innumerable instances that attest to this, among them the passionate relationship between Philip Augustus and Geoffrey or the one between Philip and Geoffrey's brother, Richard the Lionheart. Roger of Howden, a contemporary, notes that they became "inseparable" to the point that they shared food, ate from the same plate, and lay together in the same bed.[4]

Male friendships such as these generated a copious body of literature, and many texts of the period demonstrate the degree to which male bonding took precedence over heterosexuality. A prime illustration is to be found in arguably the most famous *chanson de geste* of all, *La Chanson de Roland,* which charts the legendary friendship between Roland and Oliver. This epic poem recounts how, at the pass of Roncesvalles, the rear guard of Charlemagne's army under Roland's command comes under attack by an overwhelmingly superior Saracen force. Ignoring the prudent counsel of his friend Oliver, the youthful and headstrong Roland stubbornly refuses to sound his horn to summon reinforcements. When he finally does, it is too late: despite heroic resistance, his forces are decimated, and his nobles slaughtered. Oliver is mortally wounded, and Roland himself dies in action. Charlemagne arrives on the scene only to find their corpses on the field of battle. He avenges his nephew by seeking out and killing the Saracen emir (Baligant) and executing Roland's stepfather, the treacherous Ganelon.

The Song of Roland is a typical *chanson de geste*—a stark, bloody, no-holds-barred tale of heroism and valor, of heads split open by the sword and bodies eviscerated by the lance. As the battle rages, Roland and Oliver strive to rival and surpass one another in terms of bravery. This final battle brings them even closer than before: "I recognize you, brother," says Roland, adding that "For such blows the emperor loves us."[5] The poet can scarcely contain his enthusiasm at their exploits ("If you could have seen Roland and Oliver / Hacking and hewing with their swords!").[6] But when Oliver is wounded, Roland—that paragon of courage and virility—faints clean away at the sight of his friend's "colorless, livid, pale and wan" face.[7]

They exchange parting words as Oliver dies in Roland's arms: "With these words they bowed to each other; / See how they part with such great love!"[8] Roland is disconsolate as he clutches the lifeless body of his beloved companion. In the harsh and bitter world of *The Song of Roland*, this outpouring of tenderness and brotherly love appears all the more touching. Beyond all question, this is love, as the text specifically and repeatedly describes the relationship between the two men. As Georges Duby stresses, love need in no way imply carnal knowledge but refers instead to a sentiment that goes far beyond the simple ties of friendship we know today.

The famous love celebrated between Roland and Oliver is paralleled by that of two other heroic couples in the poem, Yvon and Yvoire and Gerin and Gerer, who throughout the *Song*, are consistently described as inseparable. Both these couples also die on the field of conflict, united in death as they were in life.

The Song of Roland offers a fine example of chivalric behavior prior to the advent of a heterosexual culture in the West. That said, some commentators elect to stress the figure of Aude, Roland's fiancée, who actually puts in an appearance only toward the end of the narrative and promptly dies of a broken heart. In effect, references to Aude are contained in a meager 29 out of the poem's total of 4,002 lines, which is to say, in less than 1 percent of the whole. That said, those same 29 lines are often cited as a key passage in secondary school textbooks such as the seminal anthology of French authors compiled by Lagarde and Michard.

In his student edition of *The Song of Roland* published in 1972 as part of the canonical Classiques Larousse series, Guillaume Picot realizes how unimportant the passage really is but—presumably in a bid to address the crucial issue of love—nonetheless instructs his young readers to identify "the three principal themes" of the work as (1) depictions of feelings (love), (2) descriptions of battle, and (3) supernatural elements. Clearly, the love he alludes to is that between Roland and Aude, although he must have been seriously embarrassed to discover that the only passage open to him by way of illustration was disconcertingly short. Picot puts a bold face on it:

> Although women and love were the principal subjects of courtly literature in the twelfth and, more particularly, the thirteenth century,

these themes were rarely to be discerned in *chansons de geste*. That said, at the end of the poem, Aude (Oliver's sister and Roland's bereaved fiancée) dies after hearing the news of her loved one's demise. The passage draws its descriptive force from the very fact of its brevity and invokes comparison with similar texts that recount an all-consuming love that ends in death.[9]

Other illustrations of this "all-consuming love that ends in death" include texts relating to the tragic figures of Tristan and Iseult or to the young lovers Romeo and Juliet. Picot thus elevates Roland and Aude without further preamble to the pantheon of star-crossed lovers. Although heterosexual love rarely features in *chansons de geste* and the passage relating to Aude is brief, Picot unashamedly asserts that its impact is a function of its brevity—the shorter, evidently, the better and all the more forceful.

Picot's reading of *The Song of Roland* seeks to identify the major theme as the love between Roland and Aude, as if it were comparable to that shared by the likes of Tristan and Iseult or Romeo and Juliet, and he invites subsequent generations of students to reflect on the sublime beauty of an "all-consuming love" down through the ages. To claim that the love between Roland and Aude is central to the *Song* is highly debatable. Such groundless speculation serves only to indicate how all-pervasive our heterosexual attitudes have now become and how they generate a strong feeling of ethnocentrism. Picot's problem is not so much that *The Song of Roland* devotes significantly less time to the brief relationship between Roland and Aude than to the overarching relationship between Roland and Oliver but essentially that he deplores the presence of an "anomaly" in a benchmark work of French literature and feels that some "adjustment" is needed to purge and rehabilitate the text for the edification of future generations. In a work imbued with such historic and symbolic value, Picot clearly finds it inconvenient to alert subsequent generations to the possibility that Roland may have been less than enthusiastic about the opposite sex.

Picot's attitude is only one example among many. Numerous works of literature have been forcibly revamped for the benefit of subsequent centuries on the grounds that they were sadly at odds with the norms and conventions of heterosexual culture.

The Song of Roland was received with such enthusiasm that other writers had little hesitation in emulating its success and freely building on the saga of Roland and Oliver. In about 1180, Bertrand de Bar-sur-Aube published a prequel of sorts, a *chanson de geste* entitled *Girart de Vienne*, which, among other things, explored the origins of Roland and Oliver's indestructible friendship.[10] On the face of it, it appears that Oliver and Roland initially had all the makings of sworn enemies to the extent that one was the nephew of Charlemagne and the other the nephew of Girart, against whom Charlemagne was waging war. The two young men were the champions of the respective warring camps. Central to the plot is the subsequent 700-line scene that recounts a protracted duel between them, in the course of which Roland's admiration for his adversary slowly grows. As the duel progresses, formal civility and mutual respect increasingly give way to generosity and even tenderness. The two champions share a love of combat, and that love gradually metamorphoses into love for the opponent as the duel becomes something akin to a duet. There is magic and divine intervention in the air as the pair is enveloped in a thick cloud in which an angel appears to them, exhorting them to make their peace and join forces against the invading Saracens. Roland needs no urging:

Sir Oliver, I conceal no more
But pledge to you my loyalty,
Loving you more than any man or woman
Other than Charlemagne, my most powerful king.
Since God wishes us to be as one,
There shall be no fortress, no city,
No castle, no town, no dungeon or redoubt
That I will not share with you, if that be your desire.

Oliver's reply is instant and unequivocal:

Praise God in all His glory
That he has ordained this bond between us!
Nor do I conceal from you, Sir Roland,
That I love you more than any man born of woman.
It is my wish to give my sister's hand

And seal said contract with King Charles.
And now unlace this green and jewel-encrusted helm
That we may exchange greetings and embrace.
Roland replies: "I do so gladly."
And both shed their armor
And joyously and sincerely embrace.
Then seated side by side on the green sward.
They swear to be faithful and loyal one to the other
And to remain true friends for life.

Sitting on the grass in the middle of a meadow, seemingly oblivious to all around them, the two heroes express in word and gesture their newfound harmony. While the two opposing camps wait expectantly for the outcome of the combat, Roland and Oliver invoke divine benediction on their union and shared destiny. All is silence, time stands still—a moment of calm amid the tumult of war. It is as if the pair of them is still enveloped by the cloud sent from on high. Oliver freely pledges his sister's hand as a token of his friendship, effectively acknowledging Roland as his brother-in-law.

Aude does not appear to have been consulted in this regard, and it is a moot point whether she even has feelings for Roland. No matter: the young girl is there simply to cement the union of Roland and Oliver. She features in *Girart de Vienne* no more prominently than in *The Song of Roland*. For contemporary readers, the principal focus of both poems was on the passionate relationship between the two men rather than on that between Roland and Aude, who serves only to seal the bargain struck between them.

The course of true love does not always run smoothly, however, as is shown in the Occitan *chanson de geste* known as *Daurel and Beton*[11] dating from the close of the twelfth century. Duke Beuve de Hantone swears on the Bible and duly confirms before witnesses that, in the event of his death without issue, his worldly goods and chattels—including his widow—shall pass to Guy, his close friend of long standing. Things soon take a turn for the worse, however, when Guy starts paying court to Beuve's spouse Ermenjart. She informs her husband, who will hear none of it, refusing to think ill of his friend even when Ermenjart informs him that Guy is planning to kill him. Guy murders Beuve while they are out hunting, but not before Beuve reveals on the point of death that he would willingly have ceded his wife to Guy had he but known the depth of the latter's feeling for her. Moreover, he greatly regrets that Guy has made no such request and, with his dying breath, asks his friend to take his heart and eat it.

The tale would seem to stretch the notion of friendship to the very limit. Although Beuve has found death at Guy's hand, he nevertheless expresses the wish—in a gesture with decidedly Christlike connotations—that his friend eat his heart so that Beuve may remain with and in him throughout all eternity. The practice of eating the heart of another is a familiar enough motif in medieval literature. But one might ask what the story is intended to convey. Is it to hold up to ridicule Beuve's naiveté in refusing to believe his wife and allowing himself to be taken in by a duplicitous friend? Far from it. In fact, this is a paean to absolute and unconditional friendship. Beuve de Hantone has sworn to be Guy's friend, and he keeps his word to the very end, irrespective of the latter's betrayal. It does not even cross Beuve's mind to reproach the friend who murders him; instead, he expresses regret that he himself was not sufficiently alert and attentive to his friend's innermost desires.

And what of Ermenjart? Beuve would willingly have abandoned her to Guy—and riches and goods as well, of course. It is difficult to account for Beuve's astonishing reaction. Is Beuve blind? Hasn't it dawned on him how duplicitous Guy really is? Or does he simply find it in his heart to forgive Guy unconditionally? These and similar questions miss the point. In essence, Beuve's love for the concept of friendship is greater even than the love he feels for his friend, whom he has sworn to love until his dying day. It is this notion of unconditional friendship that captures the admiration and elevates the concept beyond that of transient relationships.

The act of giving one's wife to one's friend is less surprising than it at first appears, bearing in mind the lowly status that was enjoyed by contemporary womanhood and the unqualified esteem in which male friendship was held. This is borne out elsewhere, not least in the romance of *Athis and Procelias*,[12] where Athis is passionately in love with Prophilias (an alternate name for Procelias used in the longer version of the manuscript), who, in turn, loves Athis more than he loves his own wife and family. It so happens that Prophilias is also drawn to Cardiones, his friend's spouse, but he fears his lust may irreparably harm his friendship with Athis. As a true friend, however, Athis generously releases Cardiones, resigned to the loss not only of his spouse but also of his home, his worldly goods, and his social standing. Inevitably, perhaps, Prophilias subsequently has occasion to come to his friend's aid and save his life, confirming the passion they share for one another. According to the anonymous author, their mutual attraction is to a large extent mirrored by a physical likeness— "Alike they were in height and girth and like complexioned"[13]—which, in turn, connotes spiritual intimacy. At one point in the narrative Prophilias asks, "Am I not yours, are you not mine, and are not we two as one?"[14] Could there be any more complete expression of shared passion?

That said, the most representative work portraying the cult of friendship must surely be *Ami and Amile*, a *chanson de geste* whose popularity was reflected in the plethora of versions available in prose or verse form, in Latin, Old French, Anglo-Norman, Middle English, German, Welsh, Norse, and Old Dutch.[15]

The two protagonists are conceived by divine annunciation, born on the same day and baptized by the pope. They grow up separately. The anonymous author remarks that their physical traits and mannerisms are virtually identical: the same nose, the same mouth, the same posture at arms and in the saddle, and so on. Moreover, their beauty is beyond measure and reproach—in other words, nothing short of miraculous. Although the two young men often speak of one another, they have not met since the day of their baptism. As soon as they both come of age, however, they venture out into the wide world in the hope of finding one another. They meet at last after seven long years. Ami is on horseback. The meeting is described in stunning detail:

> Before he had gone half a league, he saw straight ahead a field that was covered with flowers as in summertime. And there he saw, astride his steed in the middle of the field, count Amile!
>
> He had never seen him, yet knew him instantly by his fine armor and all else he had heard described. With a kick of his golden spurs, he rushed toward him, and Amile, who had seen him from afar, recognized him in turn. He raced forward, and the two met in such a

tight embrace, so mighty was their kiss and so tenderly did they clasp each other, that they almost fainted dead away; their stirrups snapped and they fell together to the ground. Only now would they speak.[16]

The meadow in seasonal full flower is the *locus amoenus,* the "pleasant place" of poetic convention, the idyllic setting for what turns out to be a passionate love scene. This is a classic example of *reverdie* (literally, regreening), a poetic device commonly used in Old French texts to celebrate the arrival of spring. The two young men have found one another again after years of searching. Each instinctively recognizes the other by virtue of the fact that they are virtually mirror images, so alike as to be potentially mistaken for one another.

Picture the scene: a lone figure standing in a field, a knight in shining armor and spurs of gold, close-ups of first one face then the other, the double take as looks are exchanged, then the slow burn of mutual recognition followed by a headlong rush into one another's arms and the searing passion as they entwine in a protracted embrace. Pure Hollywood? Kitsch of the first order? Perhaps. Except for one thing: these two figures are male.

Following their reunion, Ami and Amile swear eternal love. Each duly proceeds as a matter of course to take a wife (with no impediment or contradiction implied). Their friendship is soon put to the test, however, when Charlemagne's daughter Belissant falls in love with Amile and attempts to seduce him: the couple is discovered *in flagrante* and promptly denounced to the emperor. Ami undertakes to impersonate Amile and consequently is in a position to swear by all that is holy that he has never slept with Belissant. Ami is struck down with leprosy and travels to Rome. In due course, the two friends are reunited. An angel appears and explains that Amile must sacrifice his own children and bathe Ami in their blood. Amile agrees, and Ami is immediately cured. The two then embark on a pilgrimage to the Holy Land. They die on their way home.

Ami and Amile have all the trappings of the perfect couple. Indeed, as the *ami* in their French names suggests, they are clearly intended to embody and epitomize the ideal of friendship. They are ostensibly perfect in other ways also, most notably in their identical and miraculously beautiful appearance. Their actual birth is heralded and proclaimed in advance and is reminiscent of Christ's annunciation. That Ami subsequently contracts leprosy is to be seen not as a punishment but rather as an ordeal, a test both must confront and pass. Like Abraham, Amile is willing to offer up his sons in sacrifice to save his friend. In essence, the tale starts out as a *chanson de geste* and ends up as hagiography. "Here ends the song I have sung of the good and worthy barons Ami and Amile, who gained such fame that they will be remembered until the end of time":[17] such are the last words of this sustained celebration of heroic and spiritual friendship.

The euphoria attaching to this cult of male friendship and love (the two being synonymous at the time) is constantly reflected in the incidence of near homonyms: Ami/Amile, Yvon/Yvoire, Gerin/Gerer, and Lancelot/Galehot suggest a preordained spiritual affinity—not least since proper names were considered revealing and highly significant throughout the Middle Ages. That said, similar pairings also merit mention: Floovant and Richier in the *Chanson de Guillaume*, Guillaume and Vivien in *Aliscans*, Fromont and Garin in *Garin le Loherain*, Naimes and Balan in *Aspremont*, Olivier and Fierabras in *Fierabras*, and Ogier and Karaeus in the *Chevalerie d'Ogier de Danemarche*. The examples are legion.

The prevalence of homosocial culture during the feudal period can surprise a modern public more habituated to manifestations of heterosexuality. Accordingly, it is useful to take a closer look at the nature of such male friendships, if only on the grounds that the historian, while in no position to account for specific emotions, may at the very least be permitted to comment on the historical context and social conditions that engendered them. In the present instance, the entire concept of male friendship is inextricably bound up with the specific societal structure of the age and is perhaps most readily explained by reference to four sets of social conditions.

First, feudal society was homosocial. Women were held to be of little account and, accordingly, relegated to a peripheral role, not least since they were not considered capable of arousing or experiencing deep-seated emotions. Until the emergence of courtly literature, such feelings and predilections were seen as an exclusively male preserve. *Virtus*—manly virtue and prowess—was exalted in feudal society: it was an amalgam of spiritual and physical qualities to be aspired to and emulated in every circumstance and that was central to deeply felt affinities and strongly held rivalries. The feudal knight was subject to peer-group expectations and pressures. Through good times and bad, peace and war, he and his fellow knights lived and ate as one and sometimes slept in the same bed. It was a life conducive to powerful emotions and the most indiscriminate of passions.

Second, these male *amours* were inextricably bound up with the essentially global and holistic nature of medieval society. In today's highly individualistic society, such friendships tend to be predominantly of a private nature. This was not so in the medieval world, where friendships were frequently both private and public at the same time and, moreover, socially accepted and endorsed. In other words, medieval friendships—while clearly matters of the heart—were also subject to an unwritten contract between two men where solemn oaths were sworn in the presence of witnesses, promises and pledges exchanged, mutual undertakings entered, and all manner of other social commitments acknowledged and honored. This fact goes some way toward explaining why, in certain circumstances, (male) friendship might be ordained by decree, as the author of the thirteenth-century Arthurian romance *Claris and Laris* notes. Claris and Laris are called into the presence of the king who commands them to become friends and to swear an oath of fidelity and loyalty to one another. They become inseparable, loving one another "as none had ever loved before." Indeed, the depth and extent of their love is celebrated over the course of the more than thirty thousand lines of *Claris and Laris*. (As a comparison, *Ami and Amile* is a modest 3,500 lines long.)

Third, the romance illustrates the feudal character of love between males to the extent that it is frequently governed by hierarchical considerations. The permanent presence at court of many *bacheliers*—young, unmarried bachelor knights whose services were indispensable to any sovereign lord or king intent on defending his lands and crown—inevitably spawned some measure of tension and constituted a potential source of discord and differences of opinion. That being the case, promoting stability and social cohesion often presupposed the formal encouragement of a spirit of comradeship similar to the one that allegedly obtained within the famous "Army of Lovers" in ancient Thebes. In effect, the king instructs the likes of Claris and Laris to formalize their friendship under oath in a bid to consolidate his own position. This would account for why, as noted earlier, Roland calls out to Oliver in the heat of battle: "I recognize you, brother . . . / For such blows the emperor loves us." There is thus a direct correlation between male friendship and allegiance to one's sovereign. In the case of Roland and Oliver, Charlemagne's own authority and power are effectively bolstered by the friendship between his lieutenants and their willingness to fight to the last to be worthy of each other's and their emperor's love.

Despite the fact that such male friendships directly reflect the structure and nature of feudal society, these three points should not obscure the fourth—that the emotional attachments described were intense and no less genuine for having been imposed by royal command. They represented rare pockets of tenderness and love in a world that was otherwise unremittingly brutish. The strapping hero was close to tears whenever his *compaign* (companion/lover) was threatened and would typically faint clean away should the latter be wounded or killed. A pair of lovers would hug and kiss (frequently on the lips) and often spend the night in one another's arms. Their sexual orientation was not relevant since everything they did appeared normal and natural in the eyes of their peers and contemporaries.

Courtly Literature and the Emergence of Heterosexual Culture

By the twelfth century, courtly love had become a recurrent motif in medieval society, due in no small measure to the strolling minstrels and troubadours who were obsessed with the theme. The genre was based on essentially asymmetric relationships where the female (*domina*) was the dominant figure but where social constraints represented by her husband or some villain or toady (*losengier*) conspired against the course of their true love—at which point it was sublimated in a conscious act of wish fulfillment.

At its most noble and refined, this *courtoisie* culminated in a *fin'amor* (a perfect love) that was subject to strict codes of conduct and etiquette. It was of necessity adulterous and liberating: after all, loving one's spouse might be mandatory, but to love one's lover was to exercise an option. A prospective lover was required to submit to various stages of initiation (known collectively as *assaig*) until the object of his affection consented to some form of actual physical intimacy (*sorplus*) or resolved to remain pure and chaste as befitting the ideal of *fin'amor*.

Courtly love found its expression in lyrics (*canso*), chanted to instrumental accompaniment by famous troubadour exponents such as William of Poitiers and Theobald of Champagne, as well as in the *chansons de toile* (literally, linen songs), love refrains sung by women while busy at their weaving or needlepoint. The popularity of Provençal poetry soon spread north from Occitan as Eleanor of Aquitaine and her daughter Marie de France introduced it into their respective courts in England and Champagne; its influence on romantic literature (especially the *matière de Bretagne* literary genre) was also substantial.[18]

In essence, the culture of courtly love quickly spread throughout France and beyond. Although it is not appropriate in the present context to examine the root cause of a phenomenon that to this day remains something of an enigma and continues to divide academic opinion, it perhaps suffices to stress that it postdates and in many respects clashes with the culture of male friendship. In his *Medieval Civilization*, Jacques Le Goff notes in passing that "in this period there was one feeling whose transmutation appears resolutely modern. This was love. In the more properly feudal age, with its virile, warrior society, the refinement of feelings between two beings had seemed to be confined to friendship between men."[19] Elsewhere, in his *L'Érotique des troubadours*, René Nelli adds: "The twelfth and thirteenth centuries saw love reinvent and redefine itself by assimilating the constituent rituals, mystique, and even the philosophical tenets of friendship."[20] Mention should also be made of Denis de Rougemont's attempts to identify the origins of love in the Western world.[21]

The fact is that, accustomed as they are to the logic that underpins what they regard as natural (i.e., heterosexual) culture, commentators often find it difficult to come to terms with the scope of the unprecedented revolution in medieval society triggered by the emerging concept of courtly love, as male friendships were gradually supplanted by heterosexual love. Historians such as Duby, Le Goff, and Nelli demonstrate considerable skill in charting the emergence of courtly society, but generally, they neglect what is, to my mind at least, a cardinal point: they largely ignore the decidedly confrontational transition from a feudal culture characterized by male friendships to a courtly society characterized by heterosexual love. In effect, historians generally have failed to probe the concept of heterosexuality itself—most probably because it is one they do not regard as being to any degree controversial or problematic.

The emergence and widespread acceptance of heterosexuality made life difficult for warriors, caught as they were between the bellicose ethic of chivalry—a male preserve by definition—and the dictates of courtly society. They were between two worlds—one male, one female—and at the same time forced to respond to two contradictory imperatives, reconciling their own homosocial world with an emerging heterosexual culture.

The lyrical romances of Chrétien de Troyes (c. 1135–c.1183) address this dilemma and adopt a dialectical approach to reconciling the conflicting demands of chivalric ethic and courtly society. Chrétien's early work *Erec and Enide* (c. 1170) was so successful that it was reworked both by the German author of courtly epics, Hartmann von Aue, and in the Old Norse *Erex Saga*.

Erec, son of King Lac, weds Enide, whom he loves to distraction, so much so that he ostensibly neglects his knightly obligations in favor of nightly conjugal pleasures: "But Erec was so in love with her that he cared no more for arms, nor did he go to tournaments."[22] Erec is publicly admonished on account of his weak and indolent dereliction of duty (*récréantise*) and his constant preoccupation with his wife. In other words, his manliness is called in question. Even Enide regrets that her husband is so preoccupied with her that he neglects to seek knightly glory and thus brings dishonor on both of them: "The earth should swallow me up, since the very best of knights . . . has completely abandoned all chivalry because of me."[23] She voices her feelings one night, and Erec inadvertently overhears her. Hurt, he resolves to leave for parts unknown in pursuit of fame and glory, thereby rehabilitating himself in the eyes of his spouse and demonstrating to all and sundry that he is as worthy a knight as he is devoted a husband.

Several points are worth noting, starting with the title *Erec and Enide*. On the face of it, Chrétien de Troyes is merely adhering to the widely accepted device of paronymous (like-sounding) names. Not so: up to this point, that convention had been applied to masculine pairings, such as Ami and Amile, Claris and Laris, Yvon and Yvoire, Gerin and Gerer, and so on. What is new here is that the names Erec and Enide are not both male. Cultural and literary conventions hitherto peculiar to homosocial tradition have been assimilated by analogy into heterosexual culture.

Another striking fact is that after Erec has decided to leave, his attitude to his spouse undergoes a complete change. Instead of being her devoted *chevalier servant*, he treats her virtually as if she were his page. Long-winded protestations of love are no more; he bids her be silent. In a word, he seizes the upper hand and dominates his *domina* in cavalier fashion, adopting a decidedly noncourtly stance. This suggests how difficult it was to reconcile erstwhile chivalric tradition on the one hand with the emerging principles of courtly society on the other.

The Knight with the Lion—another major work by Chrétien de Troyes—addresses the same situation, albeit in reverse. On his wedding day, Yvain tells his spouse he is impatient to leave on his adventures; she acquiesces but only on condition that he be absent for one year at most: "If you wish to have my love and if you cherish me in the least, remember to return promptly and no later than one year at most."[24]

Although Yvain initially accepts this condition, he subsequently fails to keep his word, returning later than the date originally promised to his young wife Laudine—who, as threatened, promptly rebuffs him. Distraught and driven to the point of madness, he takes to the woods, where he lives "like a madman and a savage."[25] He leaves again on his travels, eventually returning to Laudine, his true love. Yvain seems the very antithesis of Erec: valiant and uncourtly, whereas Erec is held to be courtly but not sufficiently valiant. In deserting his spouse soon after their wedding day and then staying away for more than the promised year at the outside, Yvain shows that he attaches greater importance to chivalric glory than to *courtoisie*.[26]

Chrétien's *Cligés* and *The Knight of the Cart* both seem to be straightforward celebrations of the courtly ideal, unlike *The Story of the Grail*, which again explores the dilemma outlined above. Perceval is a valiant knight, but his attitude toward women leaves something to be desired. He is less courtly than one might perhaps wish, whereas his fellow knight Gawain is extremely courtly if perhaps not quite as valiant. In their search for the elusive Grail, however, both knights are required to rise above themselves and excel in every respect. Indeed, the big and unanswered question (the narrative is sadly incomplete) is whether the two heroes are capable of doing precisely that.

The narrative romances of Chrétien de Troyes are thus preoccupied with the recurrent problem of accommodating the often contradictory demands of courtly ideal and chivalric ethos. The perfect knight is under pressure to espouse courtly values while at the same time sacrificing none of his courage and virility. Accordingly, he must strive to attain a difficult (in some cases, traumatic) compromise between the world of homosocial chivalry and the encroaching heterosexual culture of the court. Attempting to do so brings Yvain, for one, to the brink of insanity.

This tension is present not only in Chrétien's work but also in most other contemporary tales and poems. Numerous authors follow his example by addressing this classic psychological impasse, seeking to resolve what we today frequently refer to as the double blind that is implicit in well-known works such as the legend of *Tristan and Iseult*—a narrative romance that is viewed with some justification as epitomizing heterosexual culture but that actually centers less on the affirmation of the courtly ideal than on the opposition between that ideal and its chivalric counterpart.

The origins of the Tristan and Iseult legend lie in the ancient Cornwall of mythology and find expression in countless narratives on which, from the twelfth century on, successive authors attempted to impose some semblance of unity. In fact, there is not one *Tristan and Iseult* but several, each relating different episodes of the legend. Stylistic differences apart, there are a number of significant variants, including Old French narrative romances by Béroul (pre-1170) and Thomas of Britain (c. 1175), a *lai* by Marie de France entitled *Chevrefoil,* important Middle High German versions by Eilhart von Oberg and Gottfried von Strassburg, and the Old Norse *Tristrams saga ok Ísöndar.* Mention should also be made of a prose *Tristan* that appeared in France around 1230 and served as background for the celebrated *Morte d'Arthur* written more than two centuries later by the English author Sir Thomas Malory. Over the years, version succeeded version—in England, in Italy, in Portugal—and, as time passed, sundry elements were subsumed into accounts of King Arthur and his Knights of the Round Table. The Tristan legend is to be regarded not so much as an individual work than as a sort of compendium of literary inspiration down through the ages.[27]

A comparison of the versions attributed to Béroul and Thomas reveals in exemplary fashion the latter's clear shift from homosocial chivalric ethos to courtly heterosexual culture. In the Thomas version, love between a man and a woman becomes a legitimate theme in its own right, of sufficient interest to fill the pages of the entire narrative. *Adventure* is redefined as more than a tale of bellicose prowess or religious zeal or both at the same time (as, for instance, in various chronicles of the Crusades) but equates instead to the quest for love. In Béroul, the tone is less lyrical, less intense, less uplifting. There, passion is peripheral, a pretext and point of departure for a series of trials and tribulations. In the subsequent Thomas version, however, it occupies center stage in its own right.

One particular episode illustrates the difference in approach between the two versions. In Béroul, ingesting a love potion leads to the all-consuming and catastrophic passion that is Tristan's love for his uncle's intended spouse. What makes this all the more problematic is that it is not Tristan and Iseult who are the original couple but, instead, Tristan and Marc. As the opening of the Eilhart von Oberg version relates, the king holds his nephew in such great affection that he wishes only for them to be together; indeed, Marc refuses to wed, much to the consternation of his court:

> So great was his love for him [Tristan] that the king did not seek to take a wife but was resolved to look on Tristan as his son and grant him dominion over his kingdom. This greatly displeased the king's family and those of his court, who chastised him and exhorted him time and again to wed a lady of rank, but the king replied that he would countenance no such union.[28]

Taking a wife is doubtless a priority in terms of safeguarding the royal bloodline, but at the same time, there is nothing intrinsically shocking about the king's love for his young nephew, highlighting as it does the social and emotional value of vassalage in feudal society and, as some modern historians have pointed out, the singular importance of the uncle/ nephew relationship.[29]

The king's affection for his nephew is such that he is unwilling to marry, but under escalating pressure from his barons, he resorts to a subterfuge. Two swallows fly into an open window bearing a long strand of beautiful golden hair, at which point the king declares his willingness to wed the lady to whom the hair belongs, confident she can never be found. The barons voice their suspicion that Tristan is somehow behind this and is scheming to inherit Marc's crown, so Tristan solemnly undertakes to find the lady in question. Eventually he succeeds, locating Iseult and setting out to escort her to Marc's castle. They board a vessel for the journey home, and then disaster strikes. They drink the mysterious love potion, immediately triggering a conflict between, on the one hand, the homosocial relationship between king and nephew and, on the other, the heterosexual love between Tristan and Marc's intended queen. The love potion is taken in error, since the passion it arouses cannot exist other than by way of accident. Moreover, the effects of the potion wear off after three years, leaving Tristan disconsolate and closed off from Marc's court and his fellow knights, not to mention the uncle who once loved him to distraction.

The love potion appears only in the Béroul version. Thomas makes no mention of it, suggesting that Tristan and Iseult simply share a *coup de foudre*—love at first sight. No artifice is considered necessary by way of explanation: the love between them comes directly from the heart; it is spontaneous, genuine, and wholly natural. Whereas Béroul seems constrained to explain away their passion in terms of an evil spell, Thomas finds it instantly acceptable and totally without artifice. These differing interpretations are significant, revealing as they do how the powerful emotion of love has become less structured and more personal, fully in line with the notion of heterosexual love gradually supplanting the homosocial order. Seen in this light, *Tristan et Iseult* celebrates not so much what Denis de Rougemont terms the myth of love in the Western world but, instead, the triumph of heterosexual love over its homosocial counterpart.

One is tempted to say much the same thing about arguably the most famous saga of heterosexual love in medieval myth—that between Lancelot and King Arthur's wife, Guinevere.[30] In many respects, *Lancelot of the Lake* would appear to chart the confrontation between a quintessentially homosocial world and an emerging heterosexual culture.

After myriad twists and turns, the tale concludes by juxtaposing the relationships between Lancelot and the queen on the one hand and Lancelot and Galehot on the other. Galehot is in love with Lancelot: he welcomes him to his pavilion, prepares a bed for him, and announces that he (Galehot) will sleep in the adjoining chamber. After Lancelot is asleep, Galehot slips noiselessly into the young man's bed and secretly spends the night at his side ("When Galehot knew he was asleep, he lay down in the bed next to his as quietly as he could"[31]), slipping away early the next morning so that Lancelot will not suspect what has happened. As Lancelot is about to take his leave early the following day, Galehot attempts to dissuade him, promising Lancelot "all that his heart desires" should he decide to stay:

> And let me tell you that you could have the companionship of a richer man than I, but you will never have that of a man who loves you as much. And since I should do more than all the world to have your companionship, it is right that I should have it more than all the others.[32]

Lancelot agrees not to leave, albeit on one condition. If Galehot can defeat King Arthur (as everyone believes is likely given Galehot's valor and prowess in the field), then he, Galehot, shall "go to him [King Arthur] and ask his forgiveness" and put himself "utterly as his mercy."[33] Galehot agrees but insists on being loved "more than all the others." Lancelot gives an undertaking to that effect. Galehot, who has conquered no fewer than thirty kingdoms, is well placed to seize Arthur's crown—the most prized in the known world—and he succeeds in doing so despite the efforts of Gawain, that "most perfect of knights," But such is the strength of Galehot's love for Lancelot that he throws himself at the latter's feet and humbly swears obedience and loyalty to the king he has so recently defeated.

Lancelot spends the night in tears, mourning the absence of the woman he loves. Galehot attempts to console him, kissing him "on the mouth and eyes" and "comfort[ing] him energetically."[34] Queen Guinevere is anxious to see Lancelot again, and Galehot agrees to arrange a meeting, although he fears her entreaties will rob him of the person he holds most dear ("I have done so much that I am afraid your request may take from me the person I most love in the world"[35]). In an effort to reassure him, she promises to pay him back twofold for such services as he may render her. Galehot finally agrees to help and duly arranges a meeting. When he comes face to face with the queen, however, Lancelot is unaccountably bashful and tongue-tied, and it is Galehot who intercedes on behalf of his friend, imploring the queen to accept Lancelot's suit. In return, mindful of her promise, she promptly cedes Lancelot to Galehot ("I have given you Lancelot of the Lake, the son of King Ban of Benwick"[36]), at which juncture Galehot repairs to Lancelot's tent where the two spend the night in bed together, happily talking the night away: "Then Galehot left and went to his companion, and they both lay down in one bed and talked all night long of that which made their hearts content."[37]

After this emotionally charged interlude, Queen Guinevere gives Galehot (who has no female companion) to the Lady of Malehaut and makes arrangements for the four of them—herself, Malehaut, Lancelot, and Galehot—to meet every night as a foursome (so as not to arouse undue suspicion). Suddenly, Galehot announces he must take his leave, and the narrative concludes.

This concluding episode in the tale of Lancelot in no way conforms to modern expectations. Galehot's love for Lancelot is, admittedly, not unthinkable, and it is perhaps conceivable that a battle-hardened warrior like Galehot might even refrain from taking a defeated King Arthur captive by virtue of his deep affection for Lancelot. What is disconcerting, however, is that the queen, Lancelot's paramour, should negotiate with Galehot and allow him to spend the night with Lancelot and that, incredibly, having been given the royal green light to spend a night of bliss together, the two of them should do no more than talk the night away. It is also completely unexpected that Galehot should so readily consent to wed a lady not of his choosing and then leave so suddenly afterward, effectively bringing the narrative to a close (and in the process, leaving the reader thoroughly confused).

It would seem that Galehot's love for Lancelot has next to nothing in common with today's male friendships or with what we regard as homosexual relationships. There is no apparent suggestion of sodomy: a possible carnal relationship may be implied, but it is never explicit and is certainly never the principal theme. At the heart of the tale seems to lie a conventional view of an impassioned friendship between two men of a certain rank.

Conventional? Yes, but not entirely. What we have here differs from the case of Ami and Amile or that of Roland and Oliver, two examples where couples give fully of one another. In this instance, Galehot is obliged to share Lancelot with the queen. This accounts for the admixture of rivalry and cooperation that exists between Galehot and Guinevere. *Quid pro quo*, a deal is struck: Galehot conducts Lancelot to the queen, and in return, the queen gives Lancelot to Galehot. This was in line with common practice in feudal times, where personal relationships were frequently contractual in nature in the sense that one party belonged to another. Thus, a vassal was the property of his sovereign lord in much the same way as a lover was the property of his *domina*.

Lancelot du lac, published in the thirteenth century, thus celebrates not only the essence of male friendships as they obtained up to the preceding century but also the model for heterosexual love that would dominate for centuries to come.

The subtlety that permeates exchanges between the two protagonists also merits mention. Like Ami and Amile or Claris and Laris, Galehot and Lancelot have names that sound similar and that (intentionally) hint at their close personal affinity. The proper name Galehot is even closer to that of the woman he is predestined to marry (Malehaut). Yet the author makes little of this, doubtless on the grounds that he has no interest whatsoever in the heterosexual relationship between Galehot and his paronym, which is dull and insipid by comparison with the male friendships on which it is modeled. Or is it perhaps the other way round, so that the homosocial relationship between the two knights draws on notions of courtly heterosexual culture—as when Galehot, as his love for Lancelot deepens, elects at one point in the narrative to serve as Lancelot's *écuyer* (squire) in much the same way as a courtly lover would offer to serve his *domina* or lady love?

As the narrative draws to a close, the relationship between Lancelot and Guinevere seems to have taken second place to Galehot's love for Lancelot. At one point, fearing (wrongly) that his friend is dead, Galehot is so beside himself with grief that he digs his own grave—complete with a tombstone inscribed "Here lies Galehot . . . who died for love of Lancelot." When Lancelot reappears, however, the tale is taken up again, and Galehot's love is by now so intense that it has become the central theme, with the figure of Guinevere progressively marginalized and relegated to a secondary role. As the plot draws toward a conclusion of sorts, however, the eventual outcome for both couples—Lancelot and Guinevere, Lancelot and Galehot—is shrouded in vagueness and equivocation. It is as if the author is in two minds whether to opt for the homosocial or for the heterosexual rationale.

Women and Sodomy in the New Sexual Order

Tristan, Lancelot of the Lake, various works by Chrétien de Troyes, and many others attest to the stubborn resistance to heterosexual culture mounted by a previously homosocial society. Nonetheless, from the thirteenth century, the courtly ideal was by and large accorded pride of place in prose and, more particularly, in lyrical verse. This development substantially affected how women came to be portrayed and male friendships regarded.

Relative to the preceding century, the social status of women had been revised sharply upward, to the point where they were now venerated, celebrated, and courted as never before. Although a flourishing heterosexual culture had elevated them more than ever before, however, their newfound symbolic status did not necessarily equate to material advancement or equality. Quite the contrary: the twelfth and thirteenth centuries may have seen the female of the species increasingly placed on a pedestal, but at the same time, women were now open to closer scrutiny, and their conduct was subject to more stringent control and codification than previously. This may have found its most extreme expression in the form of witch hunts and sorcery trials, but even as a general rule, it was as if the true nature of the female of the species was suddenly deemed worthy of investigation. An idealized image of womanhood was developed, and women were excoriated when they failed to live up to it, even being demonized by public opinion if they failed to conform to male expectations. All in all, the cultural benefits that accrued to women were not necessarily reflected in real terms. Although this present study specifically targets heterosexual culture rather than everyday social behavior, it would certainly be invidious to neglect the social norm or be deluded into accepting it at face value.

The constraints imposed on women by courtly society are exemplified by a scene drawn from one of the anonymous *lais* or short verse romances rooted in oral tradition, the mid-thirteenth century *Lai de Graelent* in which King Arthur convenes his knights for an annual Pentecostal banquet. At the close of the banquet, he commands his lady wife to stand on the table and strip off her clothing, exposing her legendary beauty to the appreciative gaze of assembled barons and troubadours alike. Recounted as if it were entirely normal, this episode—scarcely credible to a modern audience—seems singularly at variance with what we might reasonably consider proper courtly behavior. King Arthur's ostensible boorishness tarnishes our standard image of him as the embodiment of the chivalrous ideal. Nor does the author make any apparent effort to gloss over what we might justifiably regard as an incident in, at best, extremely poor taste.

The fact remains that although the queen may well be an object of love and admiration, she remains an object. Ordered to undress, she obeys. And the king presents her for inspection in much the same way as he might exhibit a rare jewel from the royal treasury. In the process, Arthur demonstrates his own power. The queen's beauty is a yardstick by which his authority and kingship can be measured: after all, is not an uncommonly beautiful spouse his royal birthright and prerogative?

In many respects, the received notion of *courtoisie* thus reveals itself as specious and contrived, to the extent that a distinction is to be made between appearance and reality. That Arthur's queen is put on view, naked, to impress and delight the attendant knights and troubadours is wholly in line with feudal practice. A plethora of subservient soldiers, bachelor knights, equerries, and the like were in virtually permanent residence at the court and were vital if the king was to continue to assert his sovereignty and defend his crown. At the same time, however, these single males constituted a potential source of discord as sexual and social tensions inevitably mounted. Seen in this light, the queen's beauty and rank prove invaluable in keeping the wilder elements in check and helping impose some semblance of calm and order, particularly if she sees fit to bestow an occasional favor—a glance, a smile, an endearment. This all adds up to a tacit allegiance to the queen and, by extension, to the king himself—in other words, to a reaffirmation of feudal power.

It comes thus as no great surprise that, in the context of courtly society, the love the knights bear for the queen fulfills exactly the same function as that of the male friendships of the earlier period. In both instances, a potent admixture of the physical and the spiritual served to bolster a sovereign's authority. Without doubt this also goes some way toward explaining how two ostensibly incompatible notions—homosocial and heterosexual—are evidenced in such proximity and in such quick succession. The obvious clash between former homosocial traditions and the new heterosexual culture should not be underestimated, nor should it be overestimated as far as women and their social status are concerned.

Meanwhile, the burgeoning heterosexual culture led all-male relationships to be viewed increasingly as suspect. From the twelfth century, the act of sodomy was widely held to be as unnatural as heterosexual intimacy was natural (a correlation arguably based on a self-fulfilling historical premise). Moreover, in a chronological sense, the rise of heterosexual culture and the growing condemnation of homosexual practices ran broadly parallel. Contrary to widely held popular belief, the Church did not always regard sodomy as a cardinal sin. It is rarely mentioned in confessionals dating from before the twelfth century, and when it is referred to, the prescribed penance is far from severe. During the twelfth century, however, attitudes underwent radical revision, and thereafter sodomy was deemed a major capital offense.[38]

The dictates of courtly culture and the requirement that every knight be constantly at the beck and call of his lady cast a pall over the exclusively male friendships that had once seemed so natural. The upshot was that a knight who refused to espouse the new ethos of courtly love was frequently denounced as a sodomite who acted against nature. This is documented in numerous works of literature, including the late twelfth-century *lais* attributed to Marie de France, where a lady who has been rejected by Lanval (a knight at King Arthur's court) denounces him on the grounds that he must be a sodomite. Specifically, she accuses him of being averse to heterosexual pleasures and of preferring the company of handsome young men: "I well believe that you do not like this kind of pleasure. I have been told often enough that you have no desire for women. You have well-trained young men and enjoy yourself with them."[39]

In *Eneas,* a mid-twelfth-century romance that builds on Virgil's *Aeneid,* the queen explains her hatred for the hero in broadly similar terms, confiding to her daughter that Aeneas "won't eat hens but really loves the flesh of a cock. He would rather embrace a boy than you or any other woman."[40] She goes on to warn her daughter in no uncertain terms: "Daughter, you have completely lost your senses choosing such a man as your lover. He will never care about you; men who, against nature, take men and abandon women undo the natural couple. Take care that you never speak to me of him again. I urge you to give up the idea of loving this sodomite coward."[41]

It need scarcely be said that the natural law referred to here is no longer what Georges Duby identifies as the once prevalent norm governing love between two men, but rather the one that obtains between man and woman. Whereas the absence of a love potion in the Thomas of Britain version of *Tristan and Iseult* heralds the naturalizing of the man-woman relationship, the queen's outburst in *Eneas* signals its extension—a denaturalizing of male-on-male relationships. In the event, the accusations leveled in both *Lanval* and *Eneas* are unfounded and represent little more than a spiteful reaction on the part of two women who are disappointed and sexually frustrated at having been rejected. For all that, grievous damage could be done to a knight by spreading the rumor that he and his male friends engaged in sodomy, and it is equally clear that such allegations would have been ridiculed and dismissed as nonsensical as recently as a century earlier.

The knights against whom this kind of allegation was leveled found themselves in a classic double-bind situation: if they yielded to the temptations of heterosexual (courtly) love, they (like Erec) were taken to task as effeminate or recreant (that is, disloyal to the code and practice of chivalry), whereas if they elected to spurn a woman's advances, they were immediately written off as sexually deviant (like Lanval). They were between the celebrated rock and hard place.

On the whole, the emergent heterosexual culture may be said to have been resolutely opposed to male-on-male friendships (so much so that the

Eros of antiquity was now widely held to preside exclusively over man-woman relationships and no longer over relationships between men). By and large, early love theorists endorsed this view. In France, for example, Guillaume de Lorris and Jean de Meun wrote in their late thirteenth-century *Romance of the Rose* that love was a passion shared between "two persons of opposite sex,"[42] implicitly precluding love as a component of same-sex relationships. Similarly, in his benchmark treatise on the nature of courtly love—the celebrated *De Amore*, written circa 1185—Andreas Capellanus defined love as a passion proceeding from the sight of and immoderate reflection on the beauty of the other sex (*alterius sexus*). Capellanus made his point even clearer in volume 1, chapter 2, asking, "Between what persons love may exist?" and then going on to assert that "love cannot exist except between persons of opposite sexes. Between two men and two women love can find no place, for we see that two persons of the same sex are not at all fitted for giving each other the exchanges of love or for practicing the acts natural to it. Whatever nature forbids, love is ashamed to accept."[43] This point had to be driven home in the context of the transition from an erstwhile homosocial culture to a modern heterosexual society.

In any event, the pressure exerted by heterosexual culture built up over time to the point where the double-bind dilemma that was implicit in male-male companionship (and therefore sodomy) and male-female companionship (and therefore effeminacy) ultimately resolved itself as soon as courtly behavior became the norm rather than being dismissed as little more than a passing fad and an attractive alternative to the uncouth and rough-and-ready militarism that had gone before. The historical import of this change in attitude should not be underestimated.

This is best exemplified by reference to the infamous affair of the Knights Templar. On Friday, October 13, 1307, Philip IV of France (Philip the Fair) ordered the immediate and simultaneous arrest of 138 members of the Knights Templar, a monastic military order that had been founded two centuries previously soon after the First Crusade. The Templars were also bankers to whom Philip had become massively indebted. Papal inquisitor William of Paris was appointed to handle the case and bring charges of heresy and sodomy. The accused pleaded guilty to all manner of heinous crimes (most frequently under pain of torture) and a number of homosexual offenses. Seventy-six of those bought to trial admitted to sodomy but argued in their own defense that it was a practice sanctioned by statute.[44] Others pointed out that "if any natural heat should move [them],"[45] they were allowed to satisfy their needs in the company of their fellows rather than have recourse to the opposite sex. No fewer than 102 of the Paris Templars made reference to the initiation practice of "kissing the ring" (anus) and other allegedly homosexual rituals. Philip ordered further arrests throughout France (and in Castile, Aragon, Sicily, Italy, and England) as a prelude to confiscating the assets of the order and securing its dissolution. In 1310 in Paris, fifty-four Templars were burned at the stake, and many others were executed in Provence.

The affair of the Knights Templar has been the object of repeated analysis and comment. Although Philip the Fair's decision was doubtless motivated principally by political and economic considerations, the emergence of heterosexual culture by this time also helps illuminate the issue.

Whether sodomy was a regular practice among these Knights Templar is impossible to say since their confessions of guilt were obtained under torture and therefore were unreliable. But the seal of the order features two knights astride a single horse. The Templars also seem to have gone to extraordinary lengths to avoid any contact with women—curious, even in the case of a monastic order. Templar ritual allegedly also called for routine exchanges of kisses to the mouth.

These attitudes and rituals would certainly have caused a stir in 1307, but at the time when the order was founded in 1118, they would have appeared perfectly natural. A seal with two men astride a single horse? This was nothing more or less than a device illustrating chivalric friendship, a trait held in high esteem at the beginning of the twelfth century. An avowed disinclination to consort with women? This was perfectly natural in the case of monks and knights subject to codes of conduct drawn up two hundred years previously. Soldiers living together on the fringes of society? This was not unusual: that was how things were back in the bad old days of homosocial culture. But what about men kissing each other on the mouth? Didn't that constitute proof of sorts?

No, as it happens, it proved nothing. A study by Yannick Carré[46] concludes that the practice of kissing between men has a variety of connotations. It can be an indication of carnal desire (and this is how sodomites were typically portrayed in *bibles moralisées,* the so-called moralizing bibles of the age), but in most instances, it was to be construed merely as a sign of mutual friendship and shared values. It occurs frequently and publicly in epics and *chansons de geste,* as Carré most pertinently documents by reference to verses composed circa 828 in celebration of an encounter between Louis the Pious and the Pope: "Then both, the King of the Franks and the most Holy Father, took to kissing one another's eyes, lips, forehead, chest and neck." It need scarcely be added that this public exchange of kisses (*inter alia* on the lips) is to be interpreted not as symptomatic of rampant eroticism in the run-up to a night of sexual abandon but merely as one in a series of ritual gestures conveying mutual respect between two sovereigns.

As the Middle Ages drew to a close, the public exchange of male kisses on the lips became the exception rather than the rule. What had been acceptable behavior only two centuries previously was considered alien within the context of a heterosexual fourteenth-century culture, and the various rituals and values of Templar society were regarded as outdated and incomprehensible by the public at large. Men who kissed one another on the mouth were sodomites who were guilty of a crime against nature and to be excoriated accordingly.

By the early years of the fourteenth century, the clash between homosocial and heterosexual cultures had effectively been dramatically resolved. Contemporary evidence reveals that knights had increasingly no option other than to espouse the courtly ethos and pay chivalrous homage to their chosen lady. Today, the terms *chivalrous* (as opposed to *chivalric*) and *courtly* have become so close in meaning as to be virtually interchangeable. Indeed, that authoritative dictionary of the French language, *Le Grand Robert,* even defines the former in terms of the latter. In other words, whereas *chevalerie* and *courtoisie* were once antonyms, subsequent semantic usage has rendered them virtually synonymous—a clear sign of the cultural transformations that forced knights to overcome the objective contradiction that opposed the former homosocial world where they used to live in favor of the heterosexual culture that was now being pressed on them.

By the end of the Middle Ages, heterosexual culture had become the norm, although at times it faced opposition on many more fronts than can be discussed in detail in the present context. Three essential points are to be retained, however. First, Western heterosexual culture emerged in the twelfth century (as Duby, Le Goff, and a number of others have pointed out, albeit accepting it at face value and in the normal scheme of things). Second, heterosexual culture replaced an earlier homosocial culture whose influence nonetheless endured in one form or other for several centuries to come. And third, this new heterosexual culture exhibited two concomitant facts—the (fictitious) advancement of women and the (actual) condemnation and stigmatization (by both sacred and secular society) of the practice of sodomy.

2

The Renaissance: The Continuing Conflict between Homosocial Tradition and Heterosexual Culture

The onward march of heterosexual culture was everywhere in evidence during the Renaissance, not least in poetry written in the Italian manner to celebrate the peaks and troughs of courtly love. It is indicative of the age that Roland—who, in his eponymous *Chanson*, had been born into a homosocial world order and was the epitome of male heroism and a model of male friendship—should become a hero of love in Pulci's *Morgante Maggiore*, Boiardo's *Orlando innamorato*, or Ariosto's *Orlando furioso*. That Roland might fall head over heels in love with a woman would have been unthinkable in the eleventh century. However, in much the same way as new religions draw inspiration from those that have gone before and new churches come to be built where ancient temples once stood, heterosexual culture appears to have readily assimilated the heroes of the homosocial era and adapted them as it saw fit and convenient.

Reconciling Chivalry and *Courtoisie*

In both anthropological and cultural terms, the structures and institutions of medieval society continued to flourish for at least as long as the tensions between homosocial convention and heterosexual culture remained relatively pronounced. The nature of each of these two societies was such that the inherent contradictions between them would not simply disappear over the course of a couple of centuries. Instead, the conflict between them persisted from medieval times well into the Renaissance, nowhere more so than during the Italian wars.

In the context of Italy's warring city states, manly virtues rooted in the chivalric ethos were celebrated in all their former glory. Yet Italy offered a particularly sophisticated model of courtly society that the French tried to bring back home. France's monarch Francis I, in particular, attempted to reconcile Petrarchan splendor and gallantry with chivalric values. Francis was the essence of the intrepid warrior king who was well versed in all matters military and, moreover, a monarch who unhesitatingly took to the field in person, oblivious to the risks of capture (a fate, it turned out, that was to befall him in 1525). At the same time, he wrote love poems. A resolute patron of the arts, he was also instrumental in bringing Leonardo da Vinci to the French court. In a word, Francis's court embodied a synthesis between chivalry and *courtoisie*.

Francis I was thus a shining example of the new breed of courtly monarch. His particular mix of *courtoisie* and chivalry was sustained and carried forward, culminating in a court dominated by Catherine de' Medici, wife of Henry II and mother of three future kings of France (Francis II, Charles IX, and Henry III). In many eyes, this Italianate court was too courtly by far—not just profligate and shallow but also home to all manner of intrigues largely attributable to Catherine's notorious flying squadron (*escadron volant*) of young women. There were those in France and elsewhere who felt it was surely not possible to be both courtly and valiant, prompting them to ask if the typical courtier could in any event be thought of as manly or even—to put it more bluntly—as a man?

In response, French chronicler and man of letters Pierre de Bourdeille, Seigneur of Brantôme, was moved to pen an impassioned defense of France's illustrious nobles and military leaders, defending them against charges that they lacked bravery and were somewhat less than manly:

> When all is said and done, I would ask only to know what harm it does a man of action to love the ladies and partake of all the sundry pleasures and dalliances of the court? To my mind, and I have myself been privy to this in the case of many gallant men, nothing inspires a man of action more than a court and its ladies.[1]

Brantôme does not mince words. Far from being irreconcilable, a taste for war and a taste for life at court are, to his mind, wholly compatible and complementary. He goes even a step further, insisting that nothing is calculated to inspire a man of action more than a spell at court and exposure to female society generally. Indeed, he regards the ladies of the court as some sort of preparatory and motivating factor in subsequent combat. Idealization is never very far from instrumentalization.

Notwithstanding the views of Brantôme and other commentators like him, reconciling a taste for war and a taste for life at court proved to be problematic. Francis I proved fully capable of reconciling the two lifestyles, whereas over the longer term, Henry III most certainly did not.

Henry was a man of the court. Contemporary portraits attest to his Italian elegance (among other things, he wore a gold earring). He was a man of considerable erudition and a patron of the arts at a time when simplicity and sobriety were the rule. "Further," writes French historian Laurent Avezou, "during his younger bachelor days, he had engaged in a number of affairs with women, which caused the Queen Mother to say affectionately that he was 'a good stallion' whose dalliances should have produced at least one child out of wedlock."[2] In short, Henry—unlike his brother and predecessor Charles IX—was totally at ease in courtly society. But he was also a man of action, as witness his prowess at the battles of Jarnac and Montcontour. He enjoyed the military life and male companionship, surrounding himself with countless favorites who, contrary to popular belief, were quick to anger and reach for their swords on the slightest pretext. On the whole, then, one might describe Henry as comfortably homosocial within the parameters of court life.

All this changed, however, as soon as the Huguenots and, subsequently, the Catholics turned on him, leveling all manner of charges against his kingship and politics. That he put on fresh linen each day (as did the ladies of the court with whom he consorted) could only mean one thing—that he was effeminate. Paradoxically, that he was a man of action who enjoyed the company of young noblemen could only mean one thing—that he was a sodomite.

In an earlier age, an effeminate man was stereotypically held to be someone rather like Erec of *Erec and Enide*, who, as discussed earlier, was seen as altogether too courtly and suspiciously open to heterosexual relationships. The stereotypical sodomite had now come to be a man who embraced a homosocial lifestyle and enjoyed male companionship. However, since Henry III was at pains to emulate Francis I and the latter's ability to combine the homosocial and the heterosexual, Henry effectively left himself open to criticism simultaneously on both fronts. That Henry III was in all probability the first major figure in French history to be accused at one and the same time of effeminacy *and* sodomy, is something we in modern society may find astonishingly difficult to come to terms with since, as of the nineteenth century at least, the modern image of a homosexual has tended more often than not to be that of an effeminate male. Although the notion of an effeminate sodomite today appears anodyne and near-tautological, however, it must have seemed quite alien and paradoxical at the time.

Francis I, for all his Italian airs and graces, had somehow succeeded in winning the hearts and minds of his peers by virtue of being perceived and respected both at court and on the field of battle. Henry III had done his best to follow suit, but his policies had found disfavor with Huguenots and Catholics alike. Pierre de Ronsard was exceptionally scatological in his forthright condemnation of "this arse-licking sodomite king" and his "fresh-faced favorites" who allegedly "gave themselves to him day and night" and "took turns to part their buttocks to accommodate him." Elsewhere, the soldier-poet Agrippa d'Aubigné insisted that Henry was effeminate to the point where "most find it difficult to tell on first sight whether he is a female king or a male queen."

Pantagruel and Panurge

The problem of reconciling homosocial tradition and heterosexual culture was such that it featured prominently in various works of literature well into the sixteenth century. The exploits of Pantagruel and Panurge are a case in point.

Books 1 and 2 of *Gargantua and Pantagruel* are rooted in and intended as a parody of the homosocial tradition enshrined in the medieval *chanson de geste*. The Rabelaisian epic tracks the exploits of its principal—inevitably male—characters (most notably Gargantua's son Pantagruel, the so-called King of the Dipsodes) before, during, and after the phantom Picrocholine

Wars. In book 2, Rabelais recounts how Pantagruel meets Panurge, "whom he loved all his life." Shared adventures and dangers forge an enduring bond between them. As is frequently the case in most earlier chivalric epics, the first names of the two protagonists are near-homonyms (Pantagruel and Panurge), reminiscent of famous pairings such as Lancelot/Galehot, Ami/Amile, Laris/Claris, Yvon/Yvoire, Gerin/Gerer, and so on. In effect, as of book 3, this similarity is emphasized by the abbreviations employed in the narrative to indicate alternate speakers— Pant. and Pan.

The repeated expressions of the love Pantagruel bears for Panurge are consistently reprised throughout the rest of the narrative. They are inseparable. Pantagruel, the "genial giant," never ceases to be entertained by his companion's facetious wit and is always a willing participant in the latter's mischievous practical jokes. When he rebukes Panurge, he does so with infinite tenderness.

The problem of reconciling homosocial tradition and the heterosexual imperative surfaces in book 3. At the start of the novel, Pantagruel, on the advice of his father Gargantua, has taken a wife, although she never puts in an appearance, and her name is not even disclosed. Pantagruel subsequently leaves her for good and seemingly without a second thought. One might add that this is anything but courtly behavior. Indeed, unlike in *Erec and Enide,* Pantagruel's marriage is glossed over as a purely social convention and a formality of no further consequence.

Panurge's situation, on the other hand, is somewhat more complicated. With his hair going gray and his manhood beginning to show signs of wear and tear, Panurge's thoughts turn to marriage and children before it is too late. At the same time, however, he admits to a fear of marriage as an institution, certain that he will end up cuckolded or worse. Should he wed or not? To help him make up his mind, Panurge consults various oracles and authorities in matters of divination and prophecy but finds their answers disquietingly vague and confusing. He and Pantagruel finally resolve to embark on a quest to seek out and consult the ultimate authority, the tongue-in-cheek oracle of the "divine bottle" (*la dive bouteille*). Their subsequent search spawns a long series of essentially discontinuous adventures and episodic encounters with strange peoples and creatures.

In effect, the account parodies courtly convention to the extent that the latter typically comprised a sequence of rites of passage a lover was required to endure in the service of his ideal lady. In this instance, Panurge's quest is specious to the extent that one knows he will ultimately turn her down. Courtly tradition held that a knight dream of his beloved and attribute to her all manner of perfect qualities. Panurge's dream is closer to a nightmare, with the intended love object already dismissed as a "witch" and a "shrew." Clearly, Panurge has little time for the niceties of courtly behavior. He may be prepared in principle to bow to necessity and consider taking a wife, but there is no suggestion he will ever behave according to courtly tradition, billing and cooing like the Erec of old.

Gargantua and Pantagruel thus both adopts and rejects the courtly paradigm it sets out to parody and unashamedly reverts largely to the erstwhile conventions of the homosocial *chanson de geste*. The lady is here a pretext inasmuch as neither Pantagruel nor Panurge is at all interested in the opposite sex. Marriage has its place as a prelude to procreation, but genuine pleasure stems exclusively from the friendship between the two men who constitute the only couple in the novel.[3]

Humanist Drama as an Extension of Homosocial Culture

The earlier homosocial culture continued to find expression predominantly in one specific literary form, humanist drama, presumably in part because this genre was considered noble and dignified, devoted to lofty themes and exemplary protagonists, and thus perhaps less adequately served by stanzas extolling the conventions of courtly love and custom.

This is not to suggest that courtly love played no part in sixteenth-century drama, but when it did, it was generally felt that the inclusion of women had somehow weakened the plot and, at least figuratively speaking, emasculated the hero. The latter was expected to cultivate exclusively male friendships, as witness pairings such as Brutus and Collatinus or Achilles and Patroclus in plays by Nicolas Filleul,[4] Brutus and Cassius in tragedies written by Marc-Antoine Muret[5] or Jacques Grévin,[6] or David and Jonathan in the trilogy authored by Louis Des Masures.[7]

Arguably the most emblematic play of all is *Regulus* (subtitled "a tragedy based on one of the most notable events in the annals of Roman history"), published in Limoges in 1582 by one Jean de Beaubreuil, an advocate of the *présidial* or judicial tribunal. The play revolves around the heroic exploits of Regulus[8] and Manlius, two consuls of Rome, and the tragic end met by the title character, who is betrayed to and summarily executed by the Carthaginians. The entire play is awash with heroics, where fundamentally masculine values come into their own. Like medieval heroes Roland and Oliver, Ami and Amile, and Lancelot and Galehot, Manlius and Regulus are at pains to outdo one another in terms of courage in the face of the enemy. Theirs is a homosocial world of noble exploits and military derring-do, where both men excel.

As of the first scene, Atilius Regulus and Lucius Manlius give proof of their patriotism by pledging unconditional loyalty to Rome. Unlike the *fides* (oath of loyalty) sworn to one's sovereign lord in medieval times, however, this pledge is given not to an individual but to one's country. Historians have long since pointed to the sudden outpouring of patriotic sentiment that characterized sixteenth-century France,[9] and Beaubreuil's *Regulus* amply illustrates this. This new love of country surpasses all other forms of love, as Regulus proclaims: "Well may we love our families, estates, and lives, / Yet we do love this our country more, / And pledge to watch over and protect her day and night / That she may then love us in return."

To a degree, this euphoric declaration of patriotic fervor smacks of an asceticism that may help explain why there are no women whatsoever in the play: self-indulgent heterosexual love, even of the conjugal variety, has no place here. From the first scene, love remains exclusively between Atilius and Manlius, symbolized by a close embrace, an exchange of rings, a solemn pledge of a shared love so pure and complete that it cannot be undone any more than the fabled Gordian knot, coupled with a lasting commitment to serve one another as brothers. "May the Gods witness that now I love you," Atilius says. "You are my other self," Manlius answers.

This astonishing declaration of love, reiterated as act 5 opens, is an unequivocal act of faith. It is not to be confused with homosexuality (an overt admission of which would have been surprising in a sixteenth-century tragedy), but the language used is far too explicit and far too insistent to be construed as merely a token affirmation of male friendship. This is a genuine love that harks back to that expressed in antiquity by the likes of Orestes and Pylades. It is a passionate outpouring of homosocial sentiment entirely in keeping with the civic and heroic values that the play is written to celebrate.

The friendship solemnly pledged between Roland and Oliver was dedicated to their emperor Charlemagne. Here, the love that unites Manlius and Atilius is in the form of a commitment to patriotism and republicanism. The love shared by the two consuls is both a very powerful and a very political emotion.

Plots and scenes similar to the above were by no means uncommon in sixteenth-century tragedies, where virility and friendship were recurrent and popular themes. By contrast, heterosexual love often came in for critical disapproval, as in the case of *Cléopâtre captive*, the first humanist drama to be written in French. Initially performed in February 1553 at the court of Henry II, this play by Étienne Jodelle was written to commemorate Henry's heroic victory over Charles V at the siege of Metz. In it, the author portrays Mark Antony as the antithesis of the king, rendering him as a fatally flawed hero who is corrupted by erotic desire and whose manhood— as Cleopatra herself points out—has been tarnished by a "gentleness that effeminates and robs him of his strength." Anthony has effectively been stripped of his *virtus* (his manly strength) by reason of his *mollitia* or softness (effeminacy), a core concept in Roman society, where it was deemed to be symptomatic of weakness and degeneracy. In act 1, by way of illustration, Antony makes a specific allusion to his own intemperance and whoremongering, which is implicitly in contrast to the virile and valiant figure of Henry II.

Robert Garnier, beyond question the century's leading dramatist, was another who stressed the debilitating effect of *mollitia* on the heroic ethos. Like Jodelle, he also exemplifies this by reference to Mark Antony, who emerges with some credit from the first two tragedies in Garnier's Roman series—*Portia* (1568) and *Cornelia* (1574)—as commendably prudent and courageous, admirable (if arguably contrasting) qualities in the ideal hero. However, in *Mark Antony* (1578), the third and last play in Garnier's trilogy, the eponymous Antony is no longer portrayed as a valiant general and worthy successor to Caesar but, instead, as a "slave" wallowing in his passion for Cleopatra, as a direct result of which he has abandoned his wife (the sister of Octavius) and children and severed his political ties to Caesar and to Rome. Moreover, Antony's behavior not only has damaged his sense of self-worth but also—and this is infinitely more serious—has been harmful to Rome itself. In his obsessive love for the Egyptian queen, Antony has inadvertently and improperly ceded to her several possessions that should have been reserved to Rome. Worse, he has consistently brought dishonor on his native land—as Octavius forcibly reminds him in act 4. Accordingly, it is his behavior—and for Garnier, his behavior alone—that has precipitated civil war.

The clear implication is that, whereas friendship between two men might underpin the republican ideal, all-consuming love between a man and a woman can have a diametrically opposite effect and constitute a threat to the state. Egypt also suffers greatly as a direct consequence of Antony's inappropriate and distasteful liaison, which, as Philostratus observes in act 2, has wrought havoc comparable to the havoc that caused the fall of Troy. By "suckling at Cleopatra's teat," the once virtuous and valiant Antony has sacrificed public and personal values on the altar of Venus.

In all of this, there is not the slightest hint of Petrarchan empathy for the unfortunate or unrequited lover who is wounded by Cupid's arrows. In line with a certain current of antieroticism present during the Renaissance, Garnier condemns love as such.[10] Straightforward conjugal love is a necessity, but beyond that, heterosexual love may result in endangering one's country and destroying one's sense of personal honor. Where love usurps politics, heroic values are tainted, and the *res publica* is in jeopardy. Accordingly, it is unacceptable to put personal considerations before the public interest. Seen in this light, Mark Antony's dereliction of duty is to be regarded not only as delinquent and tantamount to emasculation but also as an inadmissible inversion of civic and political values.

Although tales drawn from pre-Christian history conveniently affirmed the priority of masculine and homosocial values over those of feminine and heterosexual interest, certain other examples—taken this time from Hebrew literature—also provided ammunition for sixteenth-century authors. This holds true for the biblical figure of David, who may be regarded to some degree as a mirror image of Mark Antony, not least because he starts out as a redoubtable warrior but gradually succumbs to a passion that compromises his *virtus* and leads him down the path of *mollitia*.

In 1563, Louis Des Masures published his *Tragédies saintes* (Sacred Tragedies), a trilogy based on the life of David comprising *David combattant*, *David triomphant*, and *David fugitif*. Like the majority of other works singled out for mention in the present context, the trilogy chronicles a series of heroic exploits and male friendships against the backdrop of a homosocial society. The male friendship invoked in this instance is the famous relationship between David and Jonathan. In *David triomphant*, David describes this, the sole passionate relationship of the entire trilogy, as "a sacred bond of friendship that shall never be undone,"[11] to which Jonathan responds to the effect that "this brotherly love shall endure forever"[12] and promptly offers to seal their friendship by pledging to David the hand of his sister in a gesture that is typically feudal. It is one that we have encountered before, most notably in *The Song of Roland*, where Oliver offers Roland his sister Aude's hand in marriage. In addition to celebrating the friendship between David and Jonathan, Louis Des Masures thus reveals his awareness of and indebtedness to medieval homosocial tradition.

The first part of the trilogy, *David combattant*, recounts how the Israelites address the problem of selecting a champion to oppose Goliath, the awe-inspiring Philistine giant. Jonathan volunteers, but his candidacy is swiftly rejected as is, understandably, that of King Saul himself, on the grounds that the land of Israel would be placed in dire jeopardy should he be slain. The author adheres to the biblical text where David, the youngest son of Jesse, contrives to persuade a reluctant Saul to let him fight Goliath. David readies himself for battle and approaches the giant, who mocks him and hurls a string of insults in his direction:

Is this who they send against me? A shepherd lad? Is he the one I have waited for these many days and nights? This blond-haired youngster so fresh and fair of face? Had not this stripling best douse himself in musk and myrrh and amber and make sport with the ladies? Were it not better that he toot on his whistle instead of taking the field against the likes of me? Out with it, pipsqueak! Who sends you here? Are you drunk? Or only soft in the head? Are you tired of life? Come, state your business here!

In essence, Goliath effectively transposes the physical differences between himself and David into those typical of the traditional *chanson de geste* hero on the one hand and, on the other, a *damoiseau* of no consequence—that is, a foppish young squire who has yet to earn his spurs. Goliath's choice of words reveals how little taste he has for courtly niceties. His language also hints at the scorn that humanist dramatists repeatedly poured on any show of effeminacy. The whole thrust of the play is that the boy David—for all his youth and his devotion to music and poetry—is not the spineless pipsqueak he appears to be. When all is said and done, David slays Goliath. His apparent *mollitia* is revealed as his *virtus*, his effeminacy conceals his strength.

David ou l'adultère, a play written by Antoine de Montchrestien and published in 1601, makes essentially the same point, albeit in reverse: a man of great *virtus* tragically falls prey to *mollitia*. The action centers on the well-known bible story where King David, in his determination to pay court to Bathsheba, orders her husband Uriah into battle, where the latter meets his death. As pointed out in the title of the tragedy, Montchrestien condemns not only adultery but love in general. Although the chorus chants a tribute to "chaste marriage" at the close of act 2, it is clear that love runs counter to the core values of a social order rooted in idealized masculinity.

The play opens on David, who appears to have changed beyond recognition. This King David is no longer the stripling who once bested Goliath or the mighty warrior who killed lion and bear, slew Philistine and Amalekite, defied "the princes of Ammon," and decimated "the Palestinian hordes." He is languid to the point of effeminacy. The chorus likens him to Hercules—once the world's strongest man—tamed and held in bondage to the Lydian queen Omphale and forced to do menial tasks ("women's work"), including holding wool at the ready when the queen and her handmaidens are at their spinning. Could there be any more powerful symbol of the triumph of heterosexual culture over homosocial tradition than this recurrent sixteenth-century image?

David's lapse has put his entire country at risk, as the king himself freely admits in act 1: "I have surrendered to love and abandoned my kingly duty to my country." In short, David has lost the heroic *virtus* that was once the measure and grandeur of his kingship. Uriah the Hittite betrays no such *mollitia*: he is the embodiment of exemplary masculinity, a warrior willing to devote his life to the service of his country. In act 2, Uriah forcefully rejects David's sly suggestion that he might choose to remain at home with his wife, saying: "The pleasures of the flesh are not without sin. I am a soldier, and it would be ignoble in time of war were I to seek comfort at a woman's breast." Defense of the realm must take precedence, not least over love's transient pleasures, which although perhaps conducive to happiness in marriage, can nonetheless often result in dissipation of male strength and resolve.

The primacy of heroic homosocial values over a culture of courtly love and gallantry also finds powerful expression in *L'Histoire tragique de la Pucelle de Don-Remy, autrement d'Orléans*, a play written by Father Fronton du Duc, performed initially before the nobles of the House of Lorraine on September 7, 1580, and then circulated in printed form a year later. In this instance, the values inherent in homosocial masculinity and prowess are in fact exemplified by a female, albeit in the form of Joan of Arc, the Maid of Orléans. Joan herself is alert to her unusual circumstances but asks: "Are not the armor I wear and the shield I bear more becoming than a maiden's distaff?" She is prepared to abandon her distaff (that female metaphor *par excellence*) to don armor and go off to war. She alludes to Penthesilea: if an Amazon queen could fight side by side with the Trojans, who according to legend, were the ancestors of the Franks, then why should the descendants of the latter reject out of hand the aid of a woman? She goes on to cite other examples of the instrumentality of women, including the biblical figure of Judith, who, inspired by her God and dressed in her finest garments, sets out from Bethulia (a township guarding the road to Jerusalem) to infiltrate the camp of the besieging Assyrian enemy. Judith then kills the drunken commander-in-chief Holofernes, causing such panic among the enemy that the Jews are able to rout and slaughter them.

Joan goes further, reveling in her *masle courage* (masculine bravery) and, in a scathing parody, calling into question the accepted saccharine image of femininity perpetuated by Petrarchan and Mannerist poets such as Du Bellay, Magny, Jamyn, Heroët, and so many others besides: "Let such women live without honor or glory and apart from those of us who rejoice in victory," she proclaims—"such women" being stereotypes with "rouged cheeks," "beautifully coiffed golden hair," "foreheads of ivory," "long alabaster necks," and "breasts redolent of violets, roses, and thyme."[13]

In the final analysis, the Maid's argument is to the effect that placing women on a pedestal ultimately serves only to reduce them to token objects of male fantasy and wish fulfillment. By contrast, a woman such as herself can aspire to "true" (male) military glory rather than live out such a sad and trite existence. In short, Joan rejects Venus in favor of Pallas, the Greek goddess of war. She has opted to be the equal of rather than merely different from men. Indeed, it is no exaggeration to claim she is a feminist *avant la lettre*.

It is entirely logical that, given Joan's exemplary *masle courage*, the English should be portrayed throughout in terms such as those used by Charles VII as early as act 1, scene 1: "A craven and effeminate race, a nation reeking of Arab perfume." That such creatures should dare threaten his crown is unthinkable. After the liberation of Orléans, Joan congratulates herself on having routed "this water race of vituperous and women-like cowards." In the play, it is not only the French who find the English effeminate. At the end of act 3, their commander-in-chief, the Earl of Suffolk, is incensed at the lack of *virilité* shown by his men, who flee at the sight of a woman leading the French. This virility is essential to the defense of one's country: the French appear to have it in abundance, whereas the English are cruelly bereft of it, as even their leader concedes. The paradox is that this maid exhibits exemplary *virilité*. A virgin in the mold of homosocial tradition, she rejects the demeaning and subservient role assigned to women by courtly society.

A host of similar examples can be cited in humanist drama, where heterosexual culture is challenged by homosocial tradition and the heroic ethos. The antithesis noted between chivalric and courtly literature from the twelfth century persists *mutatis mutandis* throughout the sixteenth. From the Middle Ages on, poetry came progressively under the influence of heterosexual culture, as the rise of the troubadour clearly demonstrates. This trend was continued in spectacular fashion into the Renaissance, during which a vast number of poetry collections featured the word *love* (that is, heterosexual love) in their title. In medieval times, it was perfectly acceptable to speak of the love one knight might feel for another, but this usage had largely died out by the sixteenth century. Increasingly, the term came to be used to indicate a man's love for a woman, with *friendship* used to describe a man's love for another man.

Love is the lifeblood of poetry, and poets were not slow to take advantage.[14] By the same token, however, drama—which had been given a new lease on life in the sixteenth century on the basis of classical models—continued to be regarded as a loftier pursuit and one that initially had little place for the courtly odes, idylls, and elegies that celebrated heterosexual culture.

At the end of the sixteenth century and the start of the seventeenth, heterosexual culture had begun to make headway in the theater also. Instead of the occasional one-off romantic tragedy or tragicomedy, there was suddenly a whole slew of them, notably *Isabelle* by Jean Thomas (1600), *Acoubar* by Jacques du Hamel (1603), *La Rodomontade* and *La Mort de Roger* by Charles Bauter (1603), *La Mort de Roger* (anonymous, 1605), *Tyr et Sidon* by Jean de Schélandre (1608), *Les Portugaises infortunées* and *Amnon et Thamar* by Nicolas Chrestien des Croix (1608), *Les Amours de Dalcméon et de Flore* by Estienne Bellone (1610), *Axiane* (anonymous, 1613), *Les Amours d'Angélique et de Médor* (anonymous, 1614), *Sophronie* (anonymous, 1620), *Les Amours de Zerbin et d'Isabelle* (anonymous, 1621), *Les Amours tragiques de Pyrame et Thisbé* by Théophile de Viau (1623), *Madonte* by Pierre Cottignon de la Charnays (1623), *La Mort de Bradamante, La Mort de Roger* (anonymous, 1624), and *La Charité* by M.H.L. (1624).

The titles noted above are already enough to reveal the recurrent theme of love in the Petrarchan sense, something previously unheard of in sixteenth-century humanist drama. However, they also indicate how subject matter drawn from *The Song of Roland* was being reprised, reworked, and integrated in the context of heterosexual culture—most notably in *La Rodomontade*, the three anonymous plays (two on the subject of *La Mort de Roger*, plus *Les Amours d'Angélique et de Médor* dating from 1614, and *La Mort de Bradamante*), and Garnier's *Bradamante*, the first French-language tragicomedy, dating from the final days of the sixteenth century. All these rework the *geste héroïque* of *The Song of Roland* as a romantic idyll.

French drama, until this juncture immune to the imperative of heterosexual culture, had finally succumbed.

3

The Seventeenth Century: The Triumph of Heterosexual Culture over Chivalric Opposition

The historical perspective laid out in the previous chapters should enable fresh light to be shed on the era of classic French literature and on two of its leading exponents.

Pierre Corneille

The entire *oeuvre* of French dramatist Pierre Corneille may be seen as a dialectic between disappearing homosocial values and the new and dominant heterosexual culture of courtly convention. That he was instinctively drawn to the traditional heroic ideal of virility and the sense of tragic *dignitas* is confirmed in his discourse "On the Purpose and the Parts of a Play":

The dignity of a tragedy requires some great interest of state, or some passion more noble or more manly than love, such as ambition or revenge and that inspires a fear of misfortunes greater than the loss of a mistress. It is fitting to mix love into it because love is a source of much pleasure and may serve as a basis for these interests and for these other passions of which I speak, but it [love] must be content with a secondary role in the play and leave them the primary one.

This maxim will at first seem new. It is, nonetheless, a practice of the ancients, where we see no tragedy based solely on a love interest that has to be untangled. On the contrary, they often exclude it.[1]

When he wrote the above, Corneille was fully aware that the latest fashion was for love and passion of the kind favored by dramatists such as Jean Mairet, Madeleine de Scudéry and her brother Georges, Alexandre Hardy, and many others of that ilk, but he was determined to resist the temptation to follow suit. To Corneille's mind, the virility essential to dramatic tragedy as a genre should on no account be reduced to the level of the elegiac or trite. Pointing out that "this maxim will at first seem new" is another way of saying that, in reality, it was courtly theater that was new and that threatened to dilute true drama by serving up male leads who, instead of being noble and virile, were effectively rendered effeminate by exposure to the company of women. In support of this thesis, Corneille went on to cite examples from classical drama that exhibited no interest whatsoever in love or its downstream trials and tribulations. Corneille also stressed that this notion of loveless tragedy had endured throughout the Renaissance. Accordingly, he argued, it was love interest that should be regarded as novel, just as it was love that, if accorded too great a priority, would ultimately rob tragedy of its requisite virility.

At least two distinct conclusions may be drawn from Corneille's comments. First, his approach identifies him closely with the chivalric and homosocial drama of the sixteenth century—although he acknowledges an obligation to pay lip service to the "new taste for love." Second, heterosexual culture has by now come to be regarded as so natural as to be no longer considered innovative. In his advocacy of classicism, Corneille thus appeared modernist in the eyes of his contemporaries. This is wholly indicative of how far heterosexual culture had by this time come. Having taken over the two minor literary genres of the age (poetry and the novel), it was now poised to conquer the most important genre of all—the tragedy.

To read Corneille's work is to feel how incontrovertibly his main characters are steeped in epic homosocial convention. Rodrigo, Horace, Cinna, Polyeucte, Nicomedes, Pompey, Athaliah: all are hewn from the same wood as the Roland of the *Song*. Virility is the watchword, even when its values are incorporated into a female protagonist such as Cleopatra in his *Rodogune*. Since fashion dictated there be a love interest of sorts, intrigue replaces passion, and conflicting heterosexual elements creep in and are assimilated. Thus, Rodrigo appears torn between his love for Chimène and his sense of duty (which leads him to kill her father in a duel).

The juxtaposition of homosocial tradition and heterosexual culture inherent in Corneille's body of work also goes some way toward illuminating the overt antagonism that characterized his relationship with Jean Racine. Corneille's world is one of heroic deeds and virility, with any love interest consistently relegated to the background. Racine's world may also be one of heroic deeds and *virtus*, but the essential difference is that, in his case, the love interest is of immediate and primary concern.

Jean Racine

On an initial reading of various plays by Racine, love seems to be of negligible importance. His earliest verse tragedy *The Thebaid*, for example, relates the bloody conflict between Oedipus's two sons Eteocles and Polynices and, as such, is a heroic encounter where the issue of love is of little relevance. His *Alexander the Great* deals essentially with military intrigue. His *Andromache* addresses a postwar scenario (on the face of it not immediately conducive to a study of gallantry and courtly love). His *Iphigenia* is for the most part a tale of political intrigue in time of war. His portrayal of Britannicus and Nero, that of a power struggle between two brothers at war with one another, and a retelling of the life of the all-conquering hero *Mithridates* (familiar from biographies by Plutarch and Appianus), scarcely constitutes the basis for a love story. Yet each of these serves as a point of departure and a platform for a series of amorous intrigues and subplots as Racine effectively dramatizes the subversion of homosocial and male values assimilated into heterosexual culture and courtly practice. In so doing, he distances himself radically from the approach espoused by Corneille.

That said, Racine's attitude is a shade ambiguous. It is tempting to exaggerate his preoccupation with the passion that frequently proves fatal in his plays—the erotic fury that drives a Nero, a Phaedra, or a Roxane to distraction and even to murder. In the event, he is careful to offset these cases of near madness by the interposition of foils such as Britannicus and Junia, Hippolytus and Aricia, Bajazet and Atalide, all of whom are calculated to bring tears to the eyes as models of pure and unadulterated love. In contrast to the brutal darkness of the title characters, they embody an ethereal and lyrical vision of love, and the tragic fate that lies in store for them serves only to heighten an audience's empathy. Whereas Corneille sees love as an obstacle placed in the path of a protagonist, Racine portrays the desire for power as an impediment to love. Thus, even if it is fated to end tragically, love finds recognition in Racine's *oeuvre* as a whole and, in the eyes of his audience, emerges as intrinsically and inherently beautiful.

Racine distanced himself even further from Corneille in one particular instance by electing to pen a tragedy—*Berenice*—whose theme is love itself. It is a play about love, pure and simple: no one dies tragically, and there is virtually no intrigue. It could scarcely be more anti-Corneillian. *Berenice* proved highly popular and was praised to the hilt, unlike *Titus and Berenice*, Corneille's play on essentially the same theme. Corneille had come off second best. In his later years, he made every effort to win back his place in the public's affection by injecting into his work more love interest than previously. His final play, *Suréna*, was arguably more elegiac and closer to Racine's style than any of his previous work, with a leading man who gave the appearance of being a sad and dejected victim of love: "Where is my recourse, / O Heaven, if I must always love, suffer, and die?"

It was too late. Racine and the culture of heterosexuality had long since carried the day. This would continue through the eighteenth century, with the light and flirtatious comedies of Marivaux and de Beaumarchais, then through the undiluted Romanticism of the following century, when the cult of love reached its peak in the likes of Victor Hugo's *Hernani* or Edmond Rostand's *Cyrano de Bergerac*. By the twentieth century, love had already been celebrated right across the spectrum (including in vaudeville and cabaret), and the cinema—from Marcel Carné's *Les Enfants du Paradis* to James Cameron's *Titanic*—brought it to a worldwide public, augmented by television audiences for drama series and soap operas (and even animated cartoons).

Up until the seventeenth century, homosocial tradition contrived more or less to hold its own against the tide of heterosexual culture, but from then on, the latter finally gained the upper hand once and for all. Pierre Corneille had thus mounted a despairing last-ditch defense, but it had been to no avail.

PART II

Ecclesiastical Opposition to Heterosexual Culture

What the holders of the chivalric ethic resented most about the emergent heterosexual culture was the way in which women seemed to be acquiring a significantly greater role in the overall scheme of things. The resultant increase in male effeminacy threatened to inflict grievous damage on the precious and carefully preserved fabric of homosocial society. In a word, this sudden intrusion of femininity into feudal society had provoked a crisis of gender.

When the Roman Catholic Church was called on to address the effect of the spread of courtly society, it also registered strong misgivings, but what the clergy in its turn resented above all about heterosexual culture was its sexual component. The Church feared that greater emphasis on the pleasures of the flesh might tempt the faithful from the straight and narrow and into the paths of lust and concupiscence, disrupting in the process a world order anchored in the spiritual values of the Christian faith.

The emergence of heterosexual culture was thus of the gravest concern to both church and state. To employ the terminology of French philologist and cultural historian Georges Dumézil, it appears that, albeit for different reasons, the *bellatores* and the *oratores*—those who fight and those who pray—were united in opposition to the spread of heterosexual culture.

4

The Medieval Church versus the Heterosexual Couple

Christianity was ill-placed to accommodate the notion of *courtoisie*. Christian tradition had deep roots in the image of a virgin mother who gave birth to a child who grew up celibate and who repeatedly enjoined his apostles and disciples to leave their wives and children to follow and serve the son of God.[1] In other words, the notion of man-woman relationships was a priori incompatible with Christian experience. In his First Epistle to the Corinthians, Saint Paul, coming after Jesus Christ, expressly affirms the primacy of celibacy over marriage:

> It is good for a man not to touch a woman. Nevertheless, to avoid fornication, let every man have his own wife, and let every woman have her own husband. . . . I say therefore to the unmarried and widows, It is good for them if they abide even as I. But if they cannot contain, let them marry: for it is better to marry than to burn.[2]

In sum, it would appear that marriage is something of a last resort aimed primarily at curbing concupiscence, whereas celibacy enables the faithful to take a vow of chastity before God.

Celibacy: Renouncing the Flesh, Renouncing Women

In line with Saint Paul, the Fathers of the Church and the early theologians also advocated celibacy and endorsed priesthood and the monastic life, considering woman a creature of lust to be abjured at all costs. To underpin this, countless treatises on the contemplative life, such as Philo of Alexandria's *De vita contemplativa*, were written, and innumerable sermons preached on the theme of *De contemptu saeculi* (On Contempt of the World). Hundreds of examples are to be found in French theologian Jacques-Paul Mignes' celebrated *Patrologia* alone, and virtually every author on Christianity addresses at one point or another the issue of the ascetic life (for example, the pseudo-Augustinian *Sermones ad fratres in eremo commorantes*). Father Damien also penned tracts in praise of the hermit life, the principles and merits of which he never tired of expounding, as is the case in his Opuscule 12, *De contemptu saeculi*, Op. 13, *De perfectione monachorum*, Op. 14, *De ordine eremitarum*, or Op. 51, *De vita eremitica*.

Saint Thomas was another who wrote extensively on the subject, proposing as a model the friendship between men as opposed to heterosexual relations and marriage. Meanwhile, according to Saint Jerome, the celibate Christ and the Virgin Mary had set the standard for both sexes, hence his celebrated remark—quoted time and again throughout the Middle Ages—that while "marriage replenishes the earth, virginity fills paradise."

Imposing celibacy on the priesthood was no mean feat. The injunction was formulated early on—at the beginning of the fourth century, when it appears (for example) in the canons of *concilia* such as the Synod of Elvira—but enforcing its application was another matter entirely. Many a married man managed to become a priest. Refusing the ordination of married men was a way to preserve purity, but it also meant keeping at bay men could make a useful contribution. There was no consensus on the question, and attitudes varied depending on time and place. Although the Church equivocated on this issue, throughout the Middle Ages it made every effort to elaborate rules and codes of conduct in this respect. In any event, the Second Lateran Council of 1139 definitively ruled against marriage in the case of a priest who had taken full holy orders. The clergy was enjoined to set an example in matters of the flesh and be accountable to parishioners in matters of celibacy; churchmen were threatened with excommunication should they marry secretly or indulge in heterosexual congress.[3]

Abstinence could take many forms, some brutal. In his *Travels*, Marco Polo cites the case of an old shoemaker who is visited one day by a woman of great beauty to whom he is physically attracted. Having read in his Bible that "if thine eye offend thee, pluck it out, and cast it from thee," he takes an awl and gouges his eye out. His sainthood is subsequently revealed when he (literally) moves a mountain and saves his village from marauding Saracens. In a similar vein, George Duby cites the case of a hermit called Firmat who is sorely tempted by a woman "sent by Satan" but who takes up a branding iron and sears his own flesh in a bid to fight fire with fire.[4] Overall, medieval tradition held that clerics should remain chaste and refrain from spilling either blood or semen, since, as Jacques le Goff has pointed out, "Sexual misdeeds were punished in Hell."[5]

To abstain from sex was tantamount to rejecting all women, a recommendation frequently and forcibly expressed, among others, by the tenth-century abbot Odo of Cluny:

> If men could see beneath the skin, the sight of women would make them nauseous. . . . Since we are loath to touch spittle or dung even with our fingertips, how can we desire to embrace such a sack of dung?[6]

Elsewhere, in his benchmark work *Etymologiae*, Archbishop Saint Isidore of Seville was at pains to point out that the name of the first woman on earth, Eva, was self-evidently an anagram of *vae*, the Latin word for *grief* or *misfortune*. Granted, the same three letters occurred in the Ave Maria of the Annunciation with reference to the birth of the Christ child who was destined to save all humankind. Yet most clerics continued to hold the female of the species to be injurious to the male.

The Europe of the age was monastic, and the monasteries were institutions at the sharp edge of Christianity, their duty being to convert the heathens and lead them into a state of grace. Benedictines, Franciscans, Dominicans, and monks of every denomination took it on themselves to articulate codes of behavior that prescribed a separation of the sexes. Despite some predictable sense of sexual frustration and repression at the ostracizing of womankind, canon law resolutely refused to endorse any form of behavior that was excessively natural (that is, carnal and ultimately diabolical).

Medieval Christianity may thus be seen as inimical to heterosexual culture and inclined instead toward a society of pious brotherhood and saintly predilection. This runs strangely counter to Hebraic tradition, however, inasmuch as Abraham, Isaac, and Jacob are repeatedly assured in the Old Testament that their descendants will be "as many as the stars of heaven and the grains of sand on the seashore" and that Israel's long line of patriarchs, wives, and children will "be fruitful and multiply."[7] Minor details such as these, interspersed throughout the various books of the Bible, underscored how central the issue had always been.

For the people of Israel, this preoccupation with progeny and descendants was more than merely a personal matter. Siring many sons was doubtless conducive to the continued personal economic security and social standing of the patriarchs into their old age, but it was also a geopolitical imperative. The twelve tribes of Israel were frequently ill-matched or divided among themselves. Moreover, they were comparatively small, surrounded and outnumbered by redoubtable, well-organized empires and potential enemies—Egyptians, Babylonians, Assyrians, Persians, Greeks, and others. It was vital to breed a sufficient number of soldiers to put into the field in the event of war to avoid being at serious risk of being subsumed into the Egyptian or Babylonian empire (as had previously been the case) and subjected to heathen tyranny. The promotion of a high birthrate must be seen in this light, as must the condemnation reserved in Leviticus for masturbation and homosexual congress.

Whereas Hebrew society had its anthropological roots in a culture of minimal heterosexuality (the Bible itself makes scant reference to the ups and downs of heterosexual love), the need to reproduce and multiply was considered vital in terms of what Michel Foucault once succinctly referred to as "biopower." Christian anthropology, on the other hand, was rooted in relative abnegation of sexual gratification and, to some degree, indifference to procreation. Priests, monks, and hermits were viewed as superior beings, with heterosexual love and procreation held to be inferior, vulgar, and open to reproach and censure. Some religious movements went even further. For the Cathars and Albigensians, the simple act of touching a woman, however inadvertently, constituted a mortal sin for which the penalty was severe. Although it might be said in their defense that they were simply in search of perfection, their attitude must be regarded as an extreme manifestation of the medieval Christian anthropology, which, in contradistinction to its Hebraic counterpart, was preoccupied with salvation to the detriment of procreation.

The Art of Courtly Love

A commitment to sexual abstinence was not necessarily endorsed by every Christian or by every cleric. Since the Church enjoyed a virtual monopoly of what Louis Althusser would doubtless have termed the "ideological apparatus of state" (although the state itself did not exist at the time), it was, in effect, the sole arbiter of and channel for the dissemination of spoken and written culture. As a result, the prevailing culture was anything other than what we today would regard as heterosexual.

Our focus in the present context, however, is on the culture of feudal society as opposed to broad social practice. Although social practices were more often than not defined by heterosexuality and procreational sex, cultural productions were far from being heterosexual. The Church scorned such vulgar practices and opted instead for a culture of spiritual sublimation. Proof of this abounds in Latin commentaries written throughout the Middle Ages and in early texts subsequently written in French.

Written toward the middle of the eleventh century, the *Life of Saint Alexis* is widely acclaimed as the oldest extant French-language literary text and a benchmark document in the history of French literature.[8] It recounts the life of a saint who, immediately after the wedding service, leaves his bride Émilie and sets off on a mystic voyage of self-discovery. He returns home several years later but, rather than disclose his presence, remains hidden below the stairs of the house that was once his own. He dies utterly destitute but a saint nonetheless and is in due course received into heaven by a host of angels. The thrust of the tale is self-evident: in abandoning his bride, Alexis demonstrates his preference for the celestial over the terrestrial, for heavenly as opposed to earthly love, for the spiritual over the material. Could there conceivably be a more powerful indictment of the pleasures of the flesh and of heterosexual love?

Not surprisingly, the clergy greeted the gradual emergence of a courtly culture with deep suspicion and, at times, open hostility. It found the prospect of *courtoisie* unpalatable and the thought of divine love being usurped by heterosexual love wholly unacceptable. The exigencies of courtly love were at variance with ecclesiastical doctrine, specifically where sins of the flesh were concerned. In that respect, the license now enjoyed by the troubadours could be explained away only in terms of the comparative freedom they had already acquired in practice. Although some of them were members of the Church—such as Canon Peire Cardenal or Gui Foulques, the future Pope Clement IV—troubadours had a certain degree of autonomy that often allowed them to tackle new themes. They were not fettered by the theological and pastoral tradition that dominated church literature.

The established Church was nonetheless unstinting and vociferous in its rejection of *courtoisie* and all it stood for. Sunday sermons railed against excess, debauchery, and sexual license, reserving particular condemnation not only for adultery (allegedly an essential element of courtly society) but also for the notion of heterosexual love generally, on the grounds that it was conducive to concupiscence and that it distracted men from their spiritual obligations.

In this regard, perhaps the best-known work (and possibly the most ambivalent inasmuch as it need not necessarily be taken at face value) is the twelfth-century treatise entitled *De amore* (also known as *The Art of Courtly Love*) written by Andreas Capellanus to address the new culture of eroticism. The first two books of *De amore* set out the principles of love and guidelines for their observance, and the third and final book spells out some of its shortcomings and pitfalls:

> Besides this we know beyond a doubt that God Himself is the fountainhead and origin of chastity and of modesty, and from Scripture we know that the Devil is really the author of love and lechery.[9]

The bottom line would appear to be that the kind of love celebrated by the troubadours is anathema, in grave contravention of ecclesiastical doctrine, and accordingly, to be condemned and banned under threat of excommunication. Blame attaches to women who, it seems, are (without exception) base and despicable:

> Furthermore, not only is every woman by nature a miser, but she is also envious and a slanderer of other women, greedy, a slave to her belly, inconstant, fickle in her speech, disobedient and impatient of restraint, spotted with the sin of pride and desirous of vain glory, a liar, a drunkard, a babbler, no keeper of secrets, too much given to wantonness, prone to every evil, and never loving any man in her heart.[10]

Given the above, the only union worthy of the true Christian would be spiritual as opposed to physical, as Capellanus concludes in his parting comment to Walter, his youthful interlocutor:

> Therefore, Walter, accept this health-giving teaching we offer you, and pass by all the vanities of the world, so that when the Bridegroom cometh to celebrate the greater nuptials, and the cry ariseth in the night, you may be prepared to go forth to meet Him with your lamps filled and to go in with Him to the divine marriage.[11]

The clear allusion is to the parable of the wise and foolish virgins[12] (where only the former are prepared for the bridegroom's arrival), which Capellanus adapts ostensibly to set off the eternal values of Christianity against the new and strident siren call of heterosexual culture. As intimated previously, however, the text of *De amore* is nothing if not ambiguous. Although Capellanus is at pains to condemn the excesses of courtly love, it must be admitted that the tone of the first two books is such that young Walter is unlikely to be dissuaded from his pursuit of the fairer sex. Quite the opposite: *De amore* is, to all intents and purposes, an instruction manual that outlines in considerable detail the rudiments and mechanics of successful seduction. Only much later in the work does the dialog between tutor and pupil take on a formal note of disapproval and censure.

One can only assume that Capellanus himself was aware of this incongruity. Indeed, he attempts—less than convincingly—to excuse it:

Read this little book, then, not as one seeking to take up the life of a lover but that, invigorated by the theory and trained to excite the minds of women to love, you may, by refraining from so doing, win an eternal recompense and thereby deserve a greater reward from God. For God is more pleased with a man who is able to sin and does not, than with a man who has no opportunity to sin.[13]

This smacks of sophistry. Why give instruction in the art of seduction and then counsel abstinence? In explanation, Capellanus asserts that it is because there is greater merit in choosing not to sin when one is at liberty to do so than in not sinning when one has no other option. In other words, to triumph without risk is to triumph without glory; moreover, the greater the risk, the greater the glory.

Ingenious as this rhetorically convoluted explanation may at first appear, it is essentially hypocritical rather than persuasive. The long and the short of it is that Andreas Capellanus sets out to teach the art of courtly love and goes on to do so quite effectively before finding it necessary *in extremis* to append a warning note in the interest of saving face. Rather than being an attack on courtly love, his treatise is more often than not both a thinly veiled defense and an authoritative and useful *vade mecum*.

This ambiguous and hypocritical (not to say, perverse) approach did not escape comment—all the more so since the culture of *courtoisie* was fast gaining ground. On March 7, 1277, Étienne Tempier, the ninth Bishop of Paris, took decisive action, categorically and publicly repudiating Capellanus's treatise and condemning the teaching of certain *thèses* then under debate that might appear to vindicate courtly love. In particular, the bishop formally banned promulgation of propositions that called into question the primacy of chastity. Specifically, proposition 168—*quod continentia non est essentialiter virtus* ("that abstinence is not of itself a virtue")—was overturned, as was proposition 169, *perfecta abstinentia ab actu carnis corrumpit virtutem et speciem* ("total abstinence from any act of carnality corrupts virtue and endangers the species"). Both propositions had been advanced in support of courtly love, and both were duly banned as such. The peremptory manner of their prohibition strongly suggests that the bishop viewed troubadour love poetry as more than a simple aberration: it constituted a direct challenge to the Church and to the concepts of abstinence and chastity that it had advocated for over a thousand years. The cult of heterosexual love was inimical to ecclesiastical doctrine and, in consequence, an affront to God.

As René Nelli points out, "the condemnation of 1277 bore fruit to the extent that they resulted in the virtual disappearance in France of any traces of *De amore*."[14] The belief in the primacy of the heterosexual couple did not disappear from one day to the next, but the *Condemnations* were not wholly without effect, if only to the extent that the poets of the day tended to be more circumspect in their praise of heterosexual love. Then, in 1288, Franciscan friar Matfre Ermengaud published a *Breviari d'amor*, which was markedly less ambiguous than Capellanus's *De amore* and presumably intended to reflect more accurately the opinions of the Bishop of Paris. Ermengaud's breviary expounded the view that it was perfectly admissible for a man to sing the praises of an unmarried woman, always provided that his love was honorable in the sense that it was dispassionate and accompanied by an honest intent to marry.[15] Love poetry had to be part of a prenuptial courtship ritual. This injunction was tantamount to an assault on the whole notion of courtly love since, more often than not, that love tended to be of the extraconjugal variety. If poets could sing the praises only of ladies they intended to marry, lyrical impulses were likely to dwindle away throughout the country.

Prohibition of Courtly Verse

In 1323, seven troubadours came together to draft a new code for love poetry. Their number was apposite since they intended a latter-day *pleiad*, a grouping of seven prominent practitioners modeled on that of classical antiquity (anticipating, as it turned out, a subsequent seven-star cluster during the Renaissance). Their objective was the moral regeneration of their profession in line with the dictates of the Church. To that end, they prepared the equivalent of a manifesto, but before making public the draft of *The Laws of Love* (*Les Leys d'Amors*), they had the good sense to solicit the approval of the Grand Inquisitor.

The new laws, eventually promulgated in 1356, were very clear. Anything "ugly and vile" was to be regarded as "improper" (*déshonnête*), including begging for favors, tokens, kisses, or anything else that might be construed as conducive to sin.[16] The essence of the new code was that love had to be free from sin. This was not necessarily to everyone's taste, but the draft had been accorded the Grand Inquisitor's seal of approval, had it not?

The seven contrived to leave their fellow troubadours a modest amount of room to maneuver. The best-case scenario was still that a love poem or song would be addressed to a young and unmarried maiden, providing that the intention was to seek her hand in marriage. A legitimate case could also be made for a love poem or song addressed to a married woman, not in the hope of some favor or other but exclusively with the intention of publicly celebrating her virtue, comportment, and manners and making her qualities known to a wider audience as an example for others to emulate. Legitimate as this option might be, it was also fraught with danger as a potential source of sin and, accordingly, had to be exercised with extreme caution and vigilance.

Broadly speaking, the seven troubadours were part of a movement that advocated the religious reformation of poetry. They were concerned to impose on poetry and song a measure of conformity with austere ecclesiastical doctrine and to hold in check those of their vocation whose preoccupation with courtly love appeared to have gone beyond the bounds of acceptability. They felt that poetry should not be unfettered but instead should be subject to certain rules. In short, aesthetic and ethical considerations were inseparable.

From this point, love was transformed and reformed, either in the moral or in the spiritual sense. It was surely a sign of the times that the biblical Song of Songs was increasingly the object of close study and interpretation as the perfect symbol of the mystic union between Christ and his church rather than on account of its blatantly sexual content—which was sublimated or repressed.

From the thirteenth century onward, the novelistic tradition (which played an active role in the dissemination of heterosexual culture) progressively bore the stamp of religiosity. The prose romance of *The Death of Arthur* (*La Mort le roi Artu*) is a case in point. The world of King

Arthur and his knights and their loves is coming to an end. The closing pages relate how the lone figure of Lancelot renounces all earthly love and withdraws to a monastery, takes holy orders, and devotes the rest of his days to fasting, abstinence, and self-mortification. His death is universally mourned, and he is buried in the same tomb as his beloved companion Galehot. The inscription reads: "Here lie the mortal remains of Galehot, the lord of the distant isles and, with him, the body of Lancelot of the Lake."

The pathos is intentional and designed to convey a particular notion. In chivalric eyes, Lancelot was the *prud'homme*, the paragon of integrity; from the perspective of courtly love, he was the perfect lover; but in Christian eyes, Lancelot is an adulterer who has ultimately repented and undertaken to spend the rest of his life cut off from the material world. Love is no longer in season, and heroism is a thing of the past. All that remains now is the adventure of faith and the love of God. The final touch is that Lancelot is laid to rest not next to his lady love Guinevere or his sovereign lord King Arthur but beside Galehot, the companion knight he once loved so chastely. In a sense, *The Death of Arthur* thus writes *finis* to both the age of chivalry and the age of courtly romance. It heralds the twilight of man and the dawn of the age of God.

The Sacrament of Marriage

The signs point to how poets came under increasing pressure to tailor their output to the cloth of faith. At the same time, however, the Church was making a determined effort to come to terms with heterosexual culture.

As of the start of the thirteenth century, the Church deemed it preferable to accept what it could not in practice totally prohibit: its pragmatic approach was to the effect that it was thought more advisable to accommodate than oppose. The upshot was that heterosexual love was gradually accorded the blessing of the Church, always on the condition that it would fall within ecclesiastical rules governing conjugal love.

The holy sacrament of marriage was constituted during the Fourth Lateran Council of 1215. The Church was both acknowledging the heterosexual couple and tightening its grip on the culture of love, notably through the reinforced condemnation of adultery. The blessing once pronounced jointly by the respective fathers of bride and groom was now pronounced by a single priest who had, so to speak, taken the matter in hand. At the same time, the rules governing conjugality were relaxed inasmuch as incest was henceforth held to exist in the event of consanguinity at the fourth rather than, as formerly, the seventh remove. This was some consolation, particularly for the nobility, since the earlier proscription had seriously restricted their marriage options. The link between these two measures was only too evident: redefining incest by the simple expedient of relaxing previous rules on degrees of kinship effectively extended premarital choice, whereas tightening the rules on adultery had the contrary effect of limiting postmarital access to the love market.

The decision to recognize marriage as a sacrament was far from a mere formality, and it is important to acknowledge the sacrifice made by the Church in this respect. The sacrament of priesthood had long since been recognized, together with its implicit repudiation of pleasures of the flesh. Were matrimony also to become a sacrament, however, logic required that such pleasures be tacitly recognized. The resultant ecclesiastical dilemma was not readily resolved, not least because there was also an important political dimension. If both priesthood and matrimony were sanctified, where would lie the justification for the authority of the Church over the laity, for the spiritual over the temporal? This problem had proved a thorn in the side of the Church throughout the Middle Ages, in particular during the quarrel between the Guelphs and the Ghibellines that broke out in 1215, the same year as the Fourth Lateran Council.

The stakes were high. Short of considering certain sacraments subordinate to others, elevating matrimony to sacramental status threatened to undermine the authority of the Church.

This inherent difficulty goes some way toward explaining the theological ambivalence that was to plague the Church for several centuries to come and that has arguably not been fully resolved even to this day. In effect, marriage was indeed for a long time treated as a second-tier sacrament, last in terms both of chronological order of formulation and the dignity and respect it was accorded. That said, matrimony could with some justification have been viewed as the first sacrament, bearing in mind the enforced union between Adam and Eve, in the absence of which we must all be considered their illegitimate descendants. Equally, it could be argued that the state of matrimony is arguably the most dignified and noble of all since it led to the birth of humankind and played a key role in the story of the redeemer's birth. Acknowledging matrimony as the seventh sacrament may have been risky in theological terms in that it implied recognition of the power and spread of heterosexual culture, but it was a decision that had to be taken since matrimony was the enduring symbol of the spiritual union between Christ and his church.

The problems for the Church did not end there, however. Recognition of the heterosexual couple inevitably implied acknowledgment of the new status of women, which did not sit well with an endemically misogynist Church. As Josiane Teyssot has remarked:

The [marriage] sacrament is an essential component of ecclesiastical dogma, and only those who are free and of sound mind can take part in it. It represents a potentially formidable instrument of female liberation. The Church was quick to identify the "risk" that it represented and, accordingly, since the twelfth century, looked to codify the marriage ritual and, at the same time, to foster the notion of the ideal spouse defined and limited by domesticity.[17]

Following this juncture, the Church would regularly issue tracts for the edification of young women in a bid to inform them of their duties and prerogatives within the state of Christian matrimony into which they had been welcomed. Did this imply a new status for womanhood? Symbolically, perhaps, but substantially less so in practice. Ecclesiastical dogma meant that female sexuality was now monitored even more closely than before, and in many respects, the sacrament of marriage served to modify and thereby reinforce the Christian notion of the dominant male.

In sum, the spread of heterosexual culture prompted the Church to respond in much the same way as a warrior under attack. After ages of celebrating homosocial love from which women were excluded by virtue of their gender, the warrior class endorsed the transition to courtly society and the improved standing of women implicit in the cult of *fin'amor*, but it had used it to reinforce the concept of feudal power. By the same token (and after centuries spent in celebration of the love of God and celibacy, from which women had also been excluded, this time for sexual reasons), the Church opted to endorse the sexual aspect of heterosexuality, thereby suggesting an improvement in the status of women by virtue of marriage, while at the same time using the latter sacrament as a means of shoring up its own power base. In the final analysis, however, power—whether feudal or ecclesiastical—continued, at least for the time being, to vest in men.

For Love of the Virgin Mary

The Church determined that it should go some way further in response to the perceived threat posed by heterosexual culture. It was not enough, it seemed, to proclaim that incest was to be treated more leniently and that swinging sanctions were to be imposed in respect of adultery. The Church further resolved to use as a conduit for its world view those who were arguably best placed to disseminate information to a broad public—the poets and troubadours themselves. Matfre Ermengaud and the seven troubadours responsible for drafting *The Laws of Love* had initially suggested that poets sing the praises of young maidens they were intent on marrying. Instead, poets were now enjoined by the Church to celebrate not a lady but the Lady, the Virgin Mary. The thirteenth-century Benedictine abbot Gautier de Coincy led the way, urging his fellow poets to forget the current object of their infatuation and extol instead "the One who is without equal":

> Who sings a song of love is oft cast down, and I would sing no more, yet I shall sing anew of the One of whom the angels sing.[18]

Convoluted wordplay (on the verb *chanter*, "to sing") does not obscure the point that Gautier de Coincy is intent on making here and, repeatedly, in others of his poems:

> Write, if you must, your odes and sonnets, plays and poems, songs and airs, but I shall sing only of the Holy Virgin at whose side the Son of God became a man.[19]

Elsewhere, Gautier de Coincy specifically exhorts his readers to commit to and "espouse the Virgin Mary."

Writing verses to a prospective bride was one thing, but addressing poems to the Virgin Mary another thing entirely. And although wedding a beloved woman might simply be in accord with the letter of Christian sacrament, giving oneself in marriage to the Virgin was to be seen as the ultimate gesture of love. It appears that the poets and artists of the age rushed to comply, and before long, the adoration of the Virgin was the dominant theme in poetry, painting, sculpture, and stained glass, expressed with even more fervor than that reserved to God himself.

Marian verse—poetry composed in veneration of the Virgin Mary—was a tenuous compromise between spiritual and heterosexual love. The Church was more than happy to approve of it to the extent that the female in question was divine, and the poets were more than happy to extol this divine love to the extent that its object was female. Heterosexual love thus remained hetero (although it was essentially sexless) and divine love remained divine, irrespective of the fact that it had effectively crossed the gender divide and was now directed toward the Virgin rather than toward Jesus Christ or God the Father. This compromise was to prove acceptable to both sides, although arriving at it would involve a reworking and adaptation of long-standing poetic conventions and linguistic usage. This was accomplished only with some difficulty, albeit less so in the case of those poets—among them Gautier de Coincy—who were already devout Christians or even clergymen. For others, those more reticent, a period of adjustment was needed.

One simple expedient was deliberately to cultivate ambiguity. A classic example of this is the case of poet/troubadour Bernard de Panassac, whose lyrics were so skillfully composed that it was virtually impossible to tell whether they were addressed to a lady here on earth or to the celestial Virgin Mary. Bernard de Panassac's facile permutation of the metaphysical and the overtly erotic attracted a certain amount of criticism, however, so much so that fellow poet Raimon de Cornet was led to spring to his defense and to confirm, somewhat unconvincingly, that the lady celebrated in the poem was indeed the Madonna.[20]

Ambiguity was not always the preferred solution. In many instances, it was enough to change a name here and there, expediently transforming a love poem addressed to a lady into metaphysical verse addressed to the Virgin. There are untold examples of poets recycling their own earlier compositions to produce verse in compliance with the new ground rules. This goes some way toward explaining why late medieval metaphysical poetry is at times suffused with eroticism. In the process of reworking initially secular material, certain stylistic mannerisms and immoderate metaphors were inevitably carried over.

The ambiguity favored by Bernard de Panassac and others ultimately proved an unsatisfactory solution to the problem of striking a balance between spiritual and earthly love, not least, one suspects, because his approach was manifestly opportunist and hypocritical. Once again, it was Gautier de Coincy who came up with what promised to be a viable solution in the form of the compositional technique known as *contrafacture*, whereby a vocal composition is recast by retaining the music and substituting new words. In the context of Marian devotions, however, this typically involved superimposing an imprecation to the Virgin on the melody of a popular love song, effectively substituting the secular by the sacred. It is as if Pope Benedict XVI asked a pop singer to compose a hymn to the Virgin using the melody of "My Heart Will Go On."

The *contrafacture* technique (which can also be applied in reverse) proved as popular as it was facile, prompting one anonymous poet to claim that his verse was directly inspired by the Virgin Mary:

> The sweet mother of God appeared in my dreams one summer's morn, commanding me to celebrate Her munificence in a much-loved melody, and this, by God's good grace, I did forthwith, and set fresh words to "The Nightingale's Song of Summer" in tribute to Our Lady, who brought us again into paradise once closed to us by the sins of Eve.[21]

The poem outlines the circumstances in which it was written, acknowledges the immediate source of inspiration (the Virgin), describes the compositional methodology ("fresh words," "a much-loved melody"), and incorporates conventional troubadour *topoi* ("dreams," "summer's," "Nightingale's"). Popular song has been transposed into metaphysical verse, *ars amatoria* into *ars mystica*.

As if this were not enough, however, the Church also set about sponsoring competitions to monitor how best the *contrafacture* technique might be applied to the plethora of popular love poems and songs currently in circulation, not least to ensure that their transposition into Marian verse was seemly and beyond reproach. This marked an important contribution to both artistic and spiritual reform. For example, between 1339 and 1373, the Parisian goldsmiths' guild, which already organized miracle plays every year in Notre Dame cathedral, presided over an annual poetry competition known as a *puy* (podium). Prizes were awarded to the two best poems, and these were subsequently recorded in the minutes of the guild.[22] The poetic genre in question was known in Old Occitan as the *serventois*, a form later defined by the poet Jean Molinet in his *Art de Rhétorique* of 1493 as comprising "sequences of five rhymed couplets without a refrain" and being "principally in honor of the Virgin Mary." Similar contests were held throughout France, such as during the annual floral games in Toulouse and at the Puy de Palinod competition in Rouen.

To the extent that the aim was to sublimate love rather than suppress it, Marian verse flourished toward the close of the Middle Ages. Although interpolated with Christian dogma, it was still love poetry and, as such, not very different from that of earlier troubadour generations in that it continued to celebrate female beauty, grace, and dignity (the notion of grace being particularly apposite in metaphysical poetry).

The model religious life exemplified by the homosocial and chaste spirituality of Christ and his twelve disciples had thus progressively incorporated heterosexual culture and also christianized and unsexed it. The lover was now a believer, and the lady whom he aspired to please and embrace none other than the mother of God.

Male Relationships Become Increasingly Suspect

The new openness that the Church exhibited both toward heterosexuality (always assuming it was suitably moderate and carefully monitored) and toward the token advancement of womankind as a whole (albeit within the prescribed parameters of the marriage sacrament) was offset by a progressively hostile attitude toward male relationships, which were viewed with increasing suspicion.

Such relationships had been endorsed by the philosophers of antiquity—such as by Aristotle in his *Nicomachean Ethics* and Cicero in his *De amicitia*, both cited frequently during the Middle Ages. They also had been a prominent and integral component of Christian feudal tradition exemplified—for example, by the loving tenderness that existed between Christ and Saint John and as defined in the twelfth-century *De spirituali amicitia* by Saint Ethelred of Rievaulx.

As John Boswell points out, the focus had now shifted toward sodomy and sodomites. Only a century earlier, Saint Peter Damian had dedicated to Pope Leo IX an uncompromising work entitled *The Book of Gomorrah*, which held that

Absolutely no vice can be reasonably compared with this one, which surpasses all others in uncleanness. For this vice is in fact the death of the body, the destruction of the soul; it pollutes the flesh, extinguishes the light of the mind, casts out the Holy Spirit from the temple of the human breast, and replaces it with the devil, the rouser of lust . . . it opens the doors of hell and closes the gates of heaven; it makes the citizen of the heavenly Jerusalem the heir of infernal Babylon.[23]

Peter went on to urge that any member of the clergy found guilty of sodomy be deposed from office. Pope Leo thanked him politely for his opinion and recommendations but replied that there was no need to take things to extremes. At the time, sodomy was most certainly a sin, but it was considered a minor one that was frequently glossed over and that attracted only cursory penance.

This was not so only a century later. The Church now felt it was time to take a much harder line. The Third Lateran Council held in March 1179 pronounced on sodomy, decreeing that "Whoever shall be found to have committed that incontinence that is against nature, on account of which the wrath of God came on the sons of perdition and consumed five cities with fire, shall, if a cleric, be deposed from office or confined to a monastery to do penance; if a layman, he shall suffer excommunication and be cast out from the company of the faithful."[24] By the thirteenth century, the attitude of the Church was even more draconian. Albertus Magnus and Thomas Aquinas were virulent opponents of sodomy, which in their eyes was the most despicable and arguably the most serious sin imaginable. In something less than a century, relative indifference had thus given way to thoroughgoing condemnation and calls for this "unnatural act" to be viewed as a capital offense.

The debates that took place between the eleventh and thirteenth centuries were to color Christian attitudes to sex for centuries to come. Love of God would always be seen as its noblest expression, and a believer would of necessity repudiate the pleasures of the flesh if he wished to devote his life (and his celibacy) in service to the almighty. Profane heterosexual love was also tolerated on the assumption that it was chaste (that is, conjugal) and practiced within the bonds of matrimony as redefined by holy sacrament. Male-male and female-female relationships, however, were a priori discounted: the former repudiated as sodomy, which was the mortal sin in all its splendor, and the latter regarded as perhaps of less consequence but nonetheless as a form of bestiality.

5

The Renaissance: The Enduring Conflict between the Church and Heterosexual Culture

As the Renaissance dawned, there was every indication that the Roman Catholic Church had dealt skillfully and effectively with the spread of heterosexual culture. The courtly tradition was on the wane. It was perhaps a sign of the times that Guiraut Riquier (1254–1292)—whom many historians agree to have been the last of the great troubadours—had already turned toward mysticism and against earthly pleasures, not least those of the flesh. An epoch was coming to an end.

In the France of the fourteenth and fifteenth centuries, the culture of courtly love was anything but dominant. In part, this was to be expected: the Hundred Years' War was scarcely a propitious backdrop for frivolity. As a result, the most important works of the period were mystery and morality plays, farces and *sotties* (foolishness) authored by Jean Froissart, Christine de Pizan, Alain Chartier, François Villon, Philippe de Commynes, and many others who had turned their back on their courtly heritage.

But the blaze once lit in Occitania was not totally extinguished. Far from it: it had spread across the Alps and into Italy, where Dante's *Vita Nuova* of 1294 celebrated the poet's love for Beatrice Portinari and where Laura de Noves found immortality in Petrarch's oft-imitated *Canzoniere*. From the thirteenth century onward, Italy may be said to have taken its lead from France in matters of love poetry. As of the sixteenth century, however, the reverse was true: the Renaissance in France was largely inspired by Petrarchan models and the new poetry that emerged during the Italian wars of 1494 to 1559.

Protestant Reform and the Poetry of Love

At first, it was only to be heard in the humanist city of Lyons, but soon all of France seemed awash with love poetry. The groundswell of heterosexuality that the Church had somehow contrived to stem (or at least divert) was back with a vengeance. As pointed out earlier, evidence for this resurgence is the astonishing number of contemporary collections of poems with the word *love* in their title.

To impose some semblance of order and discipline, there was recourse to the tried and tested remedy of *contrafacture*, the process by which earthly love was transposed into its celestial equivalent. As Georges Dotti has remarked:

> During the reign of Francis I, many of the most fashionable *contrafacta* were in the form of *noëls*, Christmas ballads or carols based on popular songs of the day and overlaid by religious sentiment and imagery. Leading exponents of this form included François Briand (1512), Lucas Le Moigne (c. 1520), Jehan Daniel (1524), the Lutheran Mathieu Malingre (1533), Jehan Chaperon (1538), Barthélémy Aneau (1539), and Samson Bédouin (1544). In Geneva, especially, popular songs were routinely converted into pious or polemical songs.[1]

The *noël* was a particularly apposite vehicle for contrafacture given that Christmas was a season when song—albeit often wine-induced and not necessarily always of a religious nature—could be readily adapted and infused with religious overtones. In Geneva, more than anywhere else, as Dotti points out, the essence of theological and moral reform as introduced by the Huguenots was conveyed not only in sermons and liturgical observances but also in poetry and music. *Le Droit Chemin de musique*, written in Geneva in 1550 by the French composer and music theorist Loys Bourgeois, wrote of the proper (straight and narrow) path that music should ideally take, arguing that composers should direct their talents and energies uniquely toward Christian works, most notably psalms and hymns:

It is not fitting that a true Christian compose other music. . . . Yet there are many who compose not in praise of the Lord but set to music matters abhorrent to Holy Scripture, celebrating the most awful things and polluting the noble art of composition with their lewd and vulgar ways and their loathsome and accursed execrations.

The message is unequivocal: musicians—and poets—should concentrate on producing a greater number of religious works. This did not prove particularly difficult in the case of music, since popular melodies and songs could, as Loys Bourgeois put it, simply be "appropriated into music" with the lyrics changed as necessary.

In Geneva, pressure was also mounting on painters, sculptors, and architects who, like poets and musicians, were enjoined to respect the new norm. This was particularly true in the case of poets whose work was regarded as free-thinking or even dissolute. A case in point was Theodore Beza, whose *Juvenilia* comprised sylvan idylls, elegies, portraits, epigrams, and epitaphs that marked him as arguably the leading Latin poet of the day but that also brought him into some disrepute as a libertine. In one poem, Beza wrote—on the face of it, with apparent insouciance—of his devotion to two lovers, one female (Candida) and the other male (Audebert). This and similar improprieties did not pass unnoticed. Beza was criticized and accused of debauchery and sodomy. Significantly, a second edition of the work, published in 1567 by Henri Estienne, was decidedly more circumspect. The incriminating love poems were replaced by chaste funerary laments in memory of Beza's deceased sister Madeleine and bitingly satirical anti-Catholic epigrams. Pride of place was given to pious Huguenot verse.

Beza was deemed to have paid his dues to the reformist movement and was left free to pursue his career in Geneva. When his youthful peccadilloes were forgiven and largely forgotten, in 1564 he succeeded John Calvin as head of the Académie de Genève, which was the precursor of the University of Geneva. This made him, in effect, the head of Protestantism in Switzerland and in France. This career path was extraordinary, since Geneva was widely known to have little patience with alleged debauchees and even less with sodomites (to whom the death penalty could be applied). In Beza's case, it may have been a question of words rather than deeds, but in those days, the two were often regarded as indistinguishable, especially when the written word was in the public domain and its scandalous implications caused outrage among the faithful.

It was acknowledged that Beza's poetry showed he had talent, but talent alone was not enough. To wipe the slate clean and make him palatable as a lead figure in the Protestant movement, it was vital that Beza espouse—and be seen to espouse—loftier goals. That he had once been a freethinker and libertine was useful, however, since the Church could now congratulate itself on having successfully converted a celebrated poet and peerless humanist who had once brazenly written of profane love. That history made his subsequent success even more remarkable. Genevan society was not known for its indulgence, but Beza had been deliberately rehabilitated because he was a catch—a shining example of reform.

Beza's reinstatement helped trigger a quasi-official program of literary and artistic reform in Geneva. The deteriorating political climate and the outbreak of the Wars of Religion in 1561 meant that writers had a greater role than ever before to play in matters of religion. As far back as 1550, Calvin had urged Louis Des Masures to translate the psalter. In 1562, when evangelism was at its peak in Geneva, Theodore Beza was asked to finish the work of Clément Marot, a poet and leading figure in reformist circles who had already translated some fifty psalms between 1541 and 1543. The psalms were to be set to music by various composers, among them Guillaume Franc, Guillaume Fabri, and the aforementioned Loys Bourgeois.

The psalms were an essential component of the Huguenot persuasion, and it was always the intention that the masses subsequently enjoy the fruits of this colossal editorial endeavor. Publication of the Psalter in 1562 was a major event in the religious calendar. It had proved to be a monumental task: no fewer than twenty printing houses produced the enormous number of copies that were scheduled for circulation, variously estimated at anything between thirty thousand and fifty thousand units.

Beyond this powerful message disseminated to the faithful, however, a strong signal was sent to the poets of the day that distinguished love poets such as Marot and Beza could and would be welcomed back into the bosom of the Lord. Because the Huguenots rejected the Catholic cult of sainthood and would under no circumstances worship the Virgin Mary, it was not a question of arriving at some sort of compromise between spiritual and heterosexual love. There was to be no such compromise: human love had to be renounced in favor of love of God. That was the bottom line.

What was happening in Geneva had immediate and direct implications for France. Marot and Beza, widely regarded as the two leading French and neo-Latin poets of the age, were both French by birth, and their influence was correspondingly great throughout their native France. Besides, since the inception of the reign of Francis I, Protestant reform had found a major ally in France in the guise of the king's older sister, Marguerite de Navarre, who was a writer and who presided over a large court brimming with influential personages. As a result, she was as well placed as anyone to encourage poets to reform their work, and she was fully prepared to lead the way:

Neither father, nor mother have I, nor sister nor brother, none save the God to whom I aspire. My love is not of the city, nor is it of house or castle, wife or daughter. It is only of my Savior in all His power and glory.[2]

The queen of Navarre assumed a strictly orthodox stance: the true Christian renounces not only heterosexual love but all other earthly ties, whether to father, mother, brother, or sister. Worldly concerns are of no account and (as the poem goes on to conclude), "God alone is my friend of friends, my love, my father, my mother, my brother, and my spouse." In other words, God—male and/or female at one and the same time—is the sole object of desire, and spiritual union with him is to be regarded as the only noble and worthwhile pursuit.

Marguerite de Navarre was an exponent of contrafacture, specifically designating for each poem the melodic accompaniment she had in mind, such as "to be sung to the tune of 'My Thoughts Turn Too Oft to Love'"[3] or "to the melody of 'The Thorn of My Desire.'"[4] One concrete example suffices to demonstrate how a popular lyric might be reworked from the original secular version: "A passion overwhelms me when I remember her and the verdant days of spring" was transposed into "A passion overwhelms me when I think of my God whom I cannot love enough."[5] The changes were simple but more than adequate to convey the notion of love of God that was closest to Marguerite's heart.

This was also a method that she encouraged others to adopt. Her own *valet de chambre*, Victor Brodeau, was a case in point. Brodeau was a frequent guest at gatherings of leading literary figures such as Clément Marot, Mellin de Saint-Gelais (the poet laureate of Francis I), and the cream of neo-Latin poets such as Nicolas Bourbon and the influential Jean Salmon Macrin. Brodeau had embarked on a career as a courtly poet, producing translations from the Greek and drawing inspiration largely from the fashionable neo-Petrarchans of the day. At one point, he contributed a poem entitled "Blason de la bouche" to a competition launched by Marot inviting fellow poets to write descriptive poems in praise of various parts of the female anatomy (collected and published in 1543 as *Blasons anatomiques du corps féminin*). His subsequent *Louanges de Jésus-Christ notre Sauveur* (Praise of Our Saviour Jesus Christ) and his *Épître d'un pécheur à Jésus-Christ* (A Sinner's Epistle to Jesus Christ) were markedly different in terms of style.

Other examples taken from beyond Marguerite's circle also deserve brief mention. *Les Divers Rapports*, written in 1537 by Eustorg de Beaulieu, contained a number of *risqué* (not to say decidedly ribald) passages, as a result of which the author was for a time ostracized as a good-for-nothing troublemaker. De Beaulieu decamped to Geneva and from there to Lausanne. He took holy orders and, in 1546, published 160 *contrafacta* under the collective title of *Chrestienne Resjouyssance* (Christianity Rejoices), where he consistently specifies the music that he intended to accompany his poems, in most instances taken from popular melodies of 1530 or thereabouts.

Another example is that of Agrippa d'Aubigné, whose *Hécatombe à Diane* (Sacrifice to Diana) is a striking example of the poetry of unrequited love. In his subsequent *Les Tragiques*, however, Aubigné retracts: "I write no more of an ardent love no longer known." At a time of Huguenot persecution and martyrdom, Aubigné cannot bring himself to sing the praises of Diana, so rather than invoke Hippocrene, the classical source of lyrical inspiration, he conjures up Melpomene, the muse of tragedy. But it is a tragedy that ends for the Huguenot faithful in divine revelation and a last judgment in beatitude and divine grace: "All is dead, the soul departed to find its ecstasy in the bosom of its God."

The necessary reform of heterosexual poetry proved a bone of contention between Catholics and Protestants. Pierre de Ronsard's *Discours des misères de ces temps* (A Discourse on the Miseries of This Time) famously attacked the Protestants and held them to account for the sundry disasters and afflictions that had plagued France since the outbreak of the Wars of Religion. This tirade, penned by the most prominent poet of the land, unleashed what we would today consider a veritable media storm. Reactions came thick and fast. Ronsard was pilloried in turn, particularly on the grounds that an author such as himself who had "wallowed in the concupiscent slime of love poetry"—a scathing reference to Ronsard's *Amours de Cassandre, Amours de Marie*, and *Amours d'Hélène*—was by no stretch of the imagination qualified to dispense advice when it came to matters of faith. If Huguenot pamphleteers were to be believed—and they were probably right, given how scarce copies had become—Ronsard's *Folastreries* (Follies) of 1553 had already been burnt by parliamentary decree, and Huguenots were quick to take further issue with Ronsard's "poetic debauchery" as exemplified in a mocking *Réplique* penned by Louis Des Masures writing under the pseudonym of D. M. Lescaldin,[6] which dismissed Ronsard's love poetry as that of an "ignorant and lascivious pig."

This was to prove a recurrent image, especially after another pamphlet issued by Ronsard (*Continuation au Discours sur les misères)* was followed by an impassioned *Response aux calomnies contenues en la suitte du Discours sur les Miseres de ce temps*, which described Ronsard as "one of the herd of swinish versifiers" who took no account of "the ordered invention of the ancients"[7] and whose tawdry verses and songs were on a par with those of the "youthful and misguided" Theodore Beza, who, mercifully, had since "found true ardor in God," changed his style and attitude, and gone on to "teach France how to praise God in thought and voice."[8] Admittedly, the Huguenot pamphlet noted, Beza had written licentious love poetry in his younger days, but he had since made full amends, been forgiven his youthful transgressions, and received with honor into "God's Good Grace." This Pierre de Ronsard would need to mend his ways and follow Beza's example.

The *Querelle des Discours* (as the dispute came to be known) dragged interminably on. A further libelous tract—*La Conversion de Pierre de Ronsard*—argued that Ronsard would do well to follow the example of Marot, who had been something of a libertine in his younger days but had since made amends (also by translating psalms). Beza and Marot thus emerge as two of the cultural icons of the age. Both had transgressed in their youth, but both had recognized the error of their ways, desexualized their work, and sublimated their heterosexual love poetry into a spiritual love. Ronsard represented the other side of the coin as far as his Protestant detractors were concerned. For them, he was a profligate libertine, debauchee, and unreconstructed hedonist and, as such, the opposite of Marot and Beza. He was an advocate of license and licentiousness whose love poetry was an affront to Christian sensibilities and calculated to "inflame the minds of young maidens."

In Huguenot eyes, Ronsard's behavior seemed even more scandalous and reprehensible to the extent that he had himself taken holy orders. How, they asked, could a man of God conceivably write poetry calculated to tempt young women from the straight and narrow? Wasn't that typical of the dissolute Roman Catholic Church? One pamphlet—entitled *La Métamorphose*—was written to satirize his unenviable position in this regard. It concluded that "poor Ronsard" doubtless faced a dilemma, uncertain whether to celebrate Mass or the charms of his "priestess."[9]

Catholicism and the Poetry of Love

Catholics had predictably little affection for Huguenot-inspired moral and poetical reforms. To their mind, the new and austere climate seemed more intent on abolishing earthly pleasures than on promoting celestial joy. Anti-Huguenot polemicist Florimond de Raemond was quick to mock Protestant pretensions:

> They preach certainty and truth and oppose luxury, public debauchery, and worldly follies, all of which they consider reserved to Catholic circles. They gather to neither dance nor listen to music but to read from the Bible, which is forever open on the table before them, and to sing their precious psalms, particularly ones that rhyme. The

women are modest of dress and comport themselves in public like so many plaintive Eves or repentant Magdalenes, while the menfolk go about their business with eyes cast down, mortified as if they had just espied the Holy Ghost.[10]

The fact was that substituting the spiritually uplifting "rhyming psalms" of Marot and Beza for the erstwhile libidinous and (typically) heterosexual songs usually sung at popular events and celebrations was not necessarily to everyone's taste. The poet Jacques Tahureau said as much in an amusing poem dedicated to "a young lady of a Lutheran turn of mind" who throws on the fire a copy of *Les Amours* by Jean-Antoine de Baïf on the grounds that one of his sonnets on pleasure has outraged her.[11] (In any event, De Baïf's sonnets were comparatively anodyne and certainly far from the most salacious of the period.)

To Catholic minds, this new moral fervor seemed decidedly overblown. Granted, there might be too much emphasis on the sexual aspects of male-female relationships when, at times, it might be more appropriate to preach celibacy and veneration of God and the Virgin Mary, but was there not a place for diversions and harmless pleasures? That said, Catholics were not about to cede the moral high ground to their Protestant opponents and admit they were unconcerned and less than anxious to act in matters of poetry and morality. Like the Protestants, Catholics were at pains to revamp love poetry and, wherever possible, bring its leading exponents into their camp. This was by no means easy, not least because it was impossible to condemn all love poetry for the simple reason that some of its leading exponents were actually favorites of king and court—such as Ronsard himself at the court of Henry II and Philippe Desportes at the court of Henry III. Nor should it be forgotten that both Francis I and Henry IV also wrote love poetry. Accordingly, outright prohibition of the genre was not an option. Besides, this was not Geneva.

Nevertheless—in line not only with the thinking that underpinned the Council of Trent and defined the formal position of the Catholic Church on heresy, salvation, the sacraments, and so on but also in accord with the teachings of Saint Charles Borromeo in his *Traité contre les danses et les comedies* (Treatise against Comedy and Dance)—the Catholic

Church encouraged the poets of the Renaissance to "retune their lyre" and devote their talents to God. The thinking was to demonstrate that love poetry could effectively be desexualized and that other forms of poetry were feasible, preferable, and necessary.

Sister Anne de Marquets may be said to have led by example. Her *Sonets, prieres et devises* (Sonnets, Prayers, and Devices)—written originally on the occasion of the 1561 Colloquium of Poissy and addressed to cardinals and other dignitaries attending that event—represented a last-ditch effort to reconcile Catholics and Huguenots and (perhaps) stave off the Wars of Religion. The controversial work was published in 1562 and reprinted in 1566 and set out in allegorical form the problems confronting Mother Church and pointed to their possible resolution. Sister Anne subsequently produced a compendium of *Sonets spirituels* (published posthumously) that contains no fewer than 480 poems written to elucidate the theory and practice of religious meditation. The influence of post-Tridentine reform is apparent in her work, which includes sonnets on Christmas, Ash Wednesday, the Eucharist, Assumption, Annunciation, and so on.

Anne de Marquets' output was greatly influenced by fourteenth- and fifteenth-century Marian convention, but whereas the Marian genre formerly accorded poets a degree of latitude to arrive at some form of compromise between spiritual and heterosexual love, no such freedom was on offer here. The *Sonets spirituels* were no more and no less than a virulent attack on Protestant theology, which appeared to constitute an affront to the dignity of the Virgin Mary. To that extent, Sister Anne's *oeuvre* was uncompromisingly Catholic, but the fact that she succeeded in conveying complex theological and liturgical thoughts in sonnet form, in the form that typified Petrarchan love poetry, is admirable.

The psalms posed a particularly thorny problem for Catholics when the rhymed version of the Genevan Psalter prepared by Maro and Beza became widely available and proved an important tool in attracting fresh converts to the Protestant cause. Philippe Desportes took it on himself to prepare a Catholic summary to match the enterprise of the Huguenots. This was the same Desportes whose entire life had until then been devoted to writing love poetry, notably authoring the likes of *Les Imitations de l'Arioste, Les Amours de Diane, Les Amours d'Hippolyte, Élégies, Diverses amours,* and *Dernières amours.* Desportes had since become the Abbé de Tiron, however, and was to spend the remainder of his life writing spiritual poetry, including *Cent psaumes de David* (One Hundred Psalms of David) and *Prieres et autres œuvres chrestiennes* (Prayers and Other Christian Works).

Many other names might be added to the roster of poets who were implicated in the conversion of love poetry into a more spiritual form, but caution is the watchword inasmuch as these converts were sometimes less than wholeheartedly committed. The most obvious example is arguably Joachim Du Bellay, who, like many others, opted to give up writing love poetry (such as his *L'Olive*) and seek inspiration elsewhere. In 1552, Du Bellay published a two-part collection containing several works in translation, together with a number of pieces he professed to be "of his own invention" (*Œuvres de l'invention de l'auteur*). This second part opened with an apologia entitled *Complainte du désespéré* (A Lament of the Hopeless One), in which he set out his determination "to write in celebration of God," specifically in the form of an *Israeliade* recounting in verse the history of the Jewish people. In the interim, he had written a "Christian" song that began with the following lines:

I who have so often sung the pleasures of the flesh now raise my voice in praise of an everlasting Muse. From those who wish no part in this, I seek no applause as once I did; that was my folly then, and all things have their day.

The opposition between the "carnal Muse" and the "everlasting Muse" is clearly expressed. Du Bellay dismisses the former and embraces the latter, deprecating his own erstwhile "folly" and pledging his allegiance and devotion to God. At the same time, however, he acknowledges that his choice of sacred over secular love may not be to the taste of his readership. Only a few short years later, however, Du Bellay went on to publish *Divers jeux rustiques* (Diverse Rustic Pursuits), a lighthearted verse collection that featured lovers, pretty nymphs, and tender kisses, followed by a further book of poems (*Poematum libri quatuor*) also in celebration of profane *amours.* Du Bellay's spiritual and poetical conversion had been short-lived. He had recanted and, so to speak, lapsed.

Other poets were less capricious. Gabrielle de Coignard, for one, exhibited a rare consistency in devoting her lifelong output solely to the glorification of God:

I do not desire the muse of the pagans;
Let her go to the spirits that are hers.
I am a Christian woman, burning with your flame.

And as I call your name out loud,
I lay down my all, my body, my writings, and my soul,
In the shadow of your cross.[12]

The above lines from the opening sonnet of her *Œuvres chrétiennes* constitute a clear statement of intent. Coignard is a devout Catholic who refuses to be swayed by "the muse of the pagans" and who is instead "burning" with the spiritual "flame" of Christianity. She pledges to write exclusively "in the shadow of your cross" rather than bathe in the harsh glow of carnality. Unlike Agrippa d'Aubigné, who, in his *Hécatombe à Diane* referred to earlier, elected to sacrifice a hundred bulls in gruesome tribute to his goddess, Coignard chooses to give only herself to Christ. A second sonnet reaffirms this commitment, as does her work as a whole. Much in the manner of Anne de Marquets, Coignard demonstrates that spiritual verse could be relevant to her everyday life. Her poetry may be considered as a sort of daily meditation on the practical implications of liturgy and religion as exemplified in the words of Christ and his followers.

Pious, sincere, and redolent of humility as the work of this Christian *canzoniere* most certainly is, it may come as a surprise that her last sonnet is dedicated to the memory of Pierre de Ronsard. In mourning his death, Coignard tacitly confirms that Ronsard cast a very long shadow. All her life, she had been at pains to distance herself from the fashionably pagan and erotic as celebrated by the authors of the *Pléiade*, yet she celebrates in verse the memory of one of its leading lights—Ronsard, the author of *Amours*, the *Continuation des amours*, and the *Nouvelle continuation des amours*. That Gabrielle de Coignard opted to include this closing sonnet in her *Œuvres chrétiennes* is an indication of the extent to which heterosexual culture affected the century as a whole.[13]

The Church unremittingly propagated the doctrine of divine love, although it increasingly accepted that there was a theological case of sorts to be made for heterosexuality. Overall, however, it was concerned to sustain the hierarchical distinction between spiritual and heterosexual love, between the sacred and the profane, or as described innumerable times in the literature of the age, between eros and agape, between human and divine love. This juxtaposition inspired countless painters of the age, among them (perhaps most famously) Titian, whose iconic *Sacred and Profane Love* has since occasioned much comment and interpretation—despite the fact that the title was in all probability applied retrospectively in preference to other variants.

From the thirteenth century on, the poetry of the troubadours was gradually replaced by pious Marian verse, and in the sixteenth century, Catholics and Protestants alike were intent on transforming poetry further still. Neither was to be entirely satisfied with the result. There appeared to be a residual preference for the love poetry of Marot and Du Bellay as opposed to their spiritual output. Love poetry was more popular than ever. It had secured such a firm foothold in heterosexual culture that any attempt to stem (let alone reverse) the tide was doomed to failure.

Royal Marriages and Priestly Union

Moral and theological questions posed by the spread of heterosexual culture were not limited to literary and artistic circles but also affected sociopolitical issues, some of which had been at least partially resolved in the thirteenth century, when the Church formally recognized the sacrament of marriage, thereby subsuming heterosexual culture into Christian ethics (and vice versa). But heterosexual culture developed and spread at such a rate that the issues were again raised in the sixteenth century, triggering in at least two instances unprecedented discussion and debate.

The first such instance came in the wake of the English king Henry VIII's separation from Catherine of Aragon and Pope Clement VII's subsequent refusal to grant him a divorce, at which juncture Henry and Rome went their separate ways. In 1534, with the support of Thomas Cranmer, Archbishop of Canterbury (and himself a married man at the time), the English Parliament passed the First Act of Supremacy, recognizing Henry as "the only supreme head of the church in England."

Henry's break with Rome has been the subject of repeated historical inquiry and analysis, the substance of which is not reviewed in the present context. Yet the break was primarily motivated by conjugal considerations, even if there were also political reasons. The two aspects were intricately linked. Henry had fallen in love with Anne Boleyn and was anxious to rid himself of Catherine. The Church in Rome, which had only comparatively recently instituted the holy sacrament of matrimony, could scarcely have been expected to give its blessing to the termination of a marriage by reason of what might prove a passing fancy and short-lived infatuation. Apart from essentially political considerations, Pope Clement's reluctance to accord Henry a divorce must also be attributed to the threat implicit in acknowledging the autonomy of the heterosexual couple. Granting a divorce would be tantamount to admitting that they could undermine the sacrament with impunity by the simple expedient of saying yes or no. From the point of view of the established Church, this was untenable.

On the other hand, Henry's kingship was not the gift of the Pope in Rome, and he felt himself under no obligation to submit his conjugal status to scrutiny and approval by a prelate sitting in Italy, several hundreds of miles away from his own power base in London. Henry went through the marriage and divorce cycle several times over in a sequence that is all the more remarkable since it would have been far easier and more practical to have kept a succession of mistresses rather than feel obligated to marry time and time again. Still, Henry appeared to take pleasure in marrying one mistress after another, and his tally of six marriages attests to his sovereign and inalienable independence in matters both conjugal and political.

The fact remains, however, that the marital status of one high-profile heterosexual couple had proved sufficiently controversial to provoke an ecclesiastical schism. The situation is not all that different today, when the perceived freedom of action of the heterosexual couple can be a root cause of tension between them and the Church and a matter of wider theological and pastoral concern.

In the sixteenth century, the concept of the heterosexual couple gave rise to a second and perhaps even more important focus for concern— whether priests should be permitted to marry. If matrimony was a Christian institution and sacrament, why should it not be accessible to the priesthood? The question seemed apposite, and although it was widely thought to have been addressed and answered definitively by the Second Lateran Council of 1139, it came up again at the highest level during the Renaissance. This time around, however, it divided Christianity and set lines of demarcation between Catholics and Protestants for centuries to come—even down to the present:

> The point of departure was an *Encomium matrimonii* (In Praise of Marriage), a short treatise written by Erasmus in 1519 that was reprised in several of his later colloquies. In essence, he asserted that marriage between a man and a woman, if based on mutual love and freely entered into, was more consistent with canon law than celibacy, including the *célibat consacré* of the priesthood. This approach was double-edged. To Protestants it justified rejection of ecclesiastical celibacy and virginity. . . . Every minister of the Protestant Church— Lutheran, Anglican, Reformed, and so on—would thus be free to wed, have children, and set an example of a full and productive married life.
>
> Erasmus also "discovered" that marriage can be based on *love*, whereas European society appeared to endorse marriage as a simple biological and social (i.e., procreational) necessity and to accept that "true" love did not exist other than *outside* marriage. Jean-Louis Vivès, a contemporary of Erasmus, was another staunch advocate of conjugal love and sexual congress within the bonds of matrimony. Most Catholic theologians, on the other hand, continued to go to great lengths to uphold the notion that ecclesiastical celibacy took precedence over marriage. That said, Saint Francis de Sales, the Catholic Bishop of Geneva, declared in his seminal *Introduction to the Devout Life*, that every Christian could and should have recourse to holy matrimony.[14]

The prospect of married priests reopened the debate on bachelorhood versus conjugal life. To those Catholics for whom love of God implied repudiation of the pleasures of the flesh, the state of matrimony was effectively something of a last resort. To Protestants, conversely, love between a man and a woman (and subsequent marriage) was seen as an equally noble and perhaps even more effective path to God. In his *Institutes of the Christian Religion* written in 1560, Calvin asserted that "when marriage was interdicted to priests, it was done with impious tyranny, not only contrary to the word of God, but contrary to all justice."[15]

That the reformers should have perceived no contradiction between sacred and secular love is perhaps surprising, since this bold approach appears at first glance to inject into ecclesiastical life a degree of license and sexual freedom inconsistent with the habitual intellectual rigor of Protestant reform. They did not propose reform in this area simply to make life easier for Catholics or grant free rein to lascivious noncelibate monks, however. Both Luther and his close collaborator Philip Melanchthon held celibacy to be more "worthy" than marriage but nevertheless took the view that it was an "exceptional state of grace." Moreover, they conveniently thought it a sin of pride to believe oneself capable of perpetual abstinence as ordained by decree or mandated by personal choice. To impose the rule of celibacy on every priest was therefore not only mistaken; it was the root cause of the proliferation of scandalously unchaste monks and lubricious priests who were such anathema to Huguenots and others. Was it not preferable by far—as St. Paul himself had urged—to stamp out concupiscence by channeling clerical libido into Christian matrimony?

The Protestant attitude did not stem from a sudden excess of moral and sexual permissiveness—far from it, given Luther's take on liberty as exemplified in his essay *De servo arbitrio* (The Bondage of the Will)—but was instead wholly pragmatic. It was clear that Catholic idealism and dogma might set out to enforce celibacy but that they frequently opened the door to clerical license. Protestant pragmatism, on the other hand, had the appearance of granting the clergy greater latitude. Paradoxically, it imposed even tighter control while affording both clerics and laymen an ostensibly greater amount of sexual freedom.

The debate focused yet again on the vexatious issue of how much theological and pastoral autonomy should be granted to the heterosexual couple. Catholics took the view that any proposal authorizing priests to marry ran counter to tenet and tradition, which had held since Saint Paul that celibacy and the religious life were to be preferred over conjugal love. Matrimony might well be a sacrament, they argued, but that was as far as it had been necessary to go in symbolic acknowledgment of the heterosexual couple. Authorizing the priesthood to derogate from its vows of chastity and celibacy was simply out of the question, not least since abolishing the clear hierarchy that obtained between clergy and laity implied that the two would henceforth be regarded as equals. This was a risk that could prove fatal to the established Church.

The stakes were high indeed. The sacrifice implicit in repudiation of the flesh—and by extension, matrimony—had proved essential in sustaining the moral, symbolic, and spiritual authority of the Church. It was this ascetic act of sacrifice that imparted worth and authority to the priesthood as a whole by asserting the ascendancy of spiritual power. Celibacy was thus seen as one of the major pillars on which the edifice of the Church rested; removing it would cause direct and irreparable damage. Was it not the case, ran the argument, that indulging in the pleasures of the flesh had caused humans' downfall but that their repudiation had been key to the Church's temporal authority?

Reformers such as Erasmus, Luther, Calvin, and Melanchthon could scarcely have been expected to concur. From a Catholic standpoint, preserving the institutional integrity and hierarchical authority of the Church was imperative. Reformers, on the other hand, saw scant merit in preserving an intermediate institution they regarded as flawed and tainted, advocating instead a direct relationship with God based on terms the Huguenots habitually described as *sola fide, sola gratia, sola scriptura.*[16] Protestants insisted on a "priesthood of all believers" where all Christians— laymen and clergy alike—were called into the service of an almighty God. And since all humankind was guilty of sin, there was no particular justification for standing in the way of a priest who wished to marry— quite the opposite, in fact, given that the institution of marriage was a very useful tool in regulating social and sexual behavior.

In prohibiting priests from marrying (so the argument continued), the Second Lateran Council had done them a great disservice by causing frustration and exposing them to temptation. The absurdity of prohibition had condemned them for the most part to wither and burn "under the sun of Satan."

In a bid to validate their advocacy of clerical marriage, reformist thinkers turned their attention to its lay equivalent. Erasmus, for one, wrote several dialogs and colloquies on the subject, among them "The Girl with No Interest in Marriage," in which a virginal young girl is desperately unhappy because she wishes to take holy orders instead of marrying, as her parents insist she must. Eubulus, her interlocutor, advises her:

> I'm not going to say a word against the order of nuns—though not all modes of life are equally suitable to all persons—but considering your particular temperament, which I think I've inferred from your looks and behavior, I'd urge you to marry a husband of similar tastes and establish a new community at home. Your husband would be the father of it, you the mother.[17]

Erasmus returns time and again to the notion of marriage as being in and of itself a community of Christians. He sees no need to make haste to enter a convent, given that the act of marrying and starting a family already constitutes a community. Elsewhere in the colloquy, when the girl explains how anxious she is to take a vow of chastity, Eubulus cryptically adds that "not everything's virginal among those virgins in other respects, either. . . . Because there are more who copy Sappho's behavior than share her talent."[18] For Erasmus, marriage and domesticity seem to be warranties of proper female sexuality. Convents attract both nuns and women of another persuasion.

This fresh controversy on the subject of clerical marriage went substantially beyond thirteenth-century preoccupation with the formal sacrament of marriage and the Church's attempt to postulate how an emergent heterosexual culture might formally be reconciled with established Christian doctrine and practice. The emphasis had shifted radically in the sense that now heterosexual culture was postulating ways of formally reconciling priestly behavior with the notion of conjugal love. Previously, the dominant position of the Church had allowed it to challenge the societal implications of heterosexuality. Now, the Church was in the less envious position of having to defend itself against the implications of heterosexual love in the case of the clergy. Heterosexual culture had made some significant headway, and institutional religion had been put on the defensive and forced to give ground.

Dissemination of reformist ideas beyond narrowly Protestant circles imparted growing legitimacy. The rehabilitation of marriage and (even) of conjugal love was a major feature of the age, as Sara Matthews Grieco has noted: "In terms of sexual attitudes . . . the most radical change lay in an elite reconciliation of love, sex, and marriage that was to form the basis for our concept of marriage today."[19]

It was a sign of the times that conjugal love poetry—unknown in medieval troubadour tradition—was beginning to put in a tentative appearance, most notably in the case of Jean Salmon Macrin, a disciple of Jacques Lefèvre d'Étaples and a prominent figure in the humanist circles that included the likes of polymath Guillaume Budé, Greek scholar Jean Lascaris, and neo-Latin poet Guillaume Du Bellay. Macrin authored a major work comprising not only poems glorifying God (including *An Elegy for the Dead Christ* and *Seven Psalms*) but also nuptial verse (such as his *Epithalamiorum liber unus* and *Naeniarum libri tres, de Gelonide Borsala uxore*) dedicated to his wife, Guillone Boursault. What could be more natural than to write of the love for one's spouse as well as one's love for God?

Given that he seemed disinclined to sing the praises of his own spouse, it is something of a paradox that conjugal love poetry also struck a chord with Michel de Montaigne and several of his close friends. Montaigne never tired of speaking and writing about himself, his life, his work, his personal likes and dislikes, and so on, but his wife appears almost nowhere in the pages of his remarkable *Essays*. In marked contrast is the frequent reiteration of the special affection he most famously reserved for the "sweet society" of his late young friend Étienne de La Boétie: "If you press me to say why I loved him, I feel that it cannot be expressed except by replying: 'Because it was him: because it was me.'"[20]

Such was Montaigne's grief at the premature death of his friend that he included in the first edition of the *Essays* not only the integral text of Étienne de La Boétie's seminal *Discourse of Voluntary Servitude* but also twenty-nine love poems written by La Boétie. La Boétie, it would seem, was also an exponent of conjugal verse, much of which Montaigne would go on to publish. In a letter to Marguerite de Carle discussing the lamentations of Bradamant as rendered in canto 32 of Ariosto's *Orlando furioso,* Étienne de La Boétie volunteers to translate extracts from Ariosto into French for his wife's benefit and then (rather touchingly) adds:

At your behest I would turn
Not only verse but instead
Stand the whole world on its head.

The poet Pierre de Brach, a prominent magistrate from Bordeaux, was another close friend and the person to whom Montaigne would entrust posthumous publication of the final edition of his *Essays.* De Brach published two collections of love elegies, odes and sonnets dedicated to Anne de Perrot, who would eventually become his wife. The first of his *Amours d'Aymée* were written after they first met in 1568, and the second after they married four years later. Significantly, he may be said to have followed the rules of courtship as set out variously by Matfre Ermengaud and the seven authors of the *Laws of Love* (as any self-respecting love poet should do but seldom did). Sadly, Anne died only a few years later, at which point Pierre de Brach published a collection entitled *Regrets et larmes funèbres* (Regrets and Tears of Mourning).

The case of de Brach is not particularly representative inasmuch as the vast majority of sixteenth-century love poetry was written in celebration of women who were not the poet's spouse or his intended. These few examples should suffice to show, however, that love poetry addressed to a spouse was a comparatively recent development in the genre. It served to demonstrate that love of God was not incompatible with heterosexual love and, at the same time, that—when all was said and done—heterosexual love was not incompatible with marriage.

6

The Seventeenth Century: The Triumph of Heterosexual Culture over Ecclesiastical Opposition

The seventeenth century saw the Roman Catholic Church still locked in battle against the steady advance of a heterosexual culture that was perceived to be progressively propagating license and eroding ecclesiastical authority. It was accepted that poetry had fallen prey to the cult of love, but the novel still remained, admittedly a lesser known literary form in the preceding century but now fêted in the *salons* of Paris and increasingly popular among women, where titles such as *Amadis*, *L'Astrée*, *Clélie*, and *Pharamond* were all the rage. Many of these novels were voluminous, and some were racy swashbuckling tales that captivated an expanding readership.

A man reading this kind of love story might run the risk of being accused of a certain *mollitia* injurious to his image of masculinity and knightly perfection (not unlike the hapless Don Quixote, for example). For the Church, however, this was not the primary concern. Men rarely read these novels (they were left to women), and besides, the Church was not especially interested in the warrior ethos. The fact that men could read novels was essentially a gender issue, whereas the problem for the Church lay elsewhere—namely, in the issue of sex. Accordingly, women readers were thought to be at grave risk of being infected by a kind of *impudicitia* or sexual impurity that was prejudicial to their femininity and contrary to their so-called natural calling.

Leading clergymen, alarmed at the threat posed by the novel, were not slow to initiate a program of pedagogical reform. In his *L'Honneste femme* (translated as *The Compleat Woman*), for instance, Father Jacques du Bosc identified what was at stake:

> Inasmuch as we deem it improper for mothers to expose themselves— let alone their offspring—to certain paintings, is it not evident that the lascivious content of the novel will do similar harm to their imagination and leave its stain on their soul? That reading such novels will make women bold and brash, shrewish, conniving and prone to sly evil-doing? . . . Have we not seen how some will leave their native hearth and family to run after some stranger or other of whom they have suddenly become amorous? Or how others welcome love letters penned by admirers, and others still consent to furtive assignations? These novels are nought but insidious manuals of artifice and sin.[1]

There was no denying that novels were liberally sprinkled with examples of ruse and artifice that might be regarded as potentially harmful to young and innocent minds. Novel reading was not without danger: the heroine who started as a virgin could easily end up a debauchee. This was a threat that came to be perceived as progressively acute as the novel form became more popular.

The Theater of Religion versus the Theater of Love

Although the novel was an increasingly controversial literary form, the Church's real quarrel in the seventeenth century was with the theater. This was for several reasons. First, there was a great deal at stake, given that theatergoing was the quintessential social ritual of the age. The court would attend *en masse*, and performances were sometimes graced by the presence of the king himself. Further—and this was particularly true in the provinces—widespread illiteracy meant that strolling players could reach audiences immeasurably larger than the potential novel-reading public. Finally, the theater had proved largely immune to the cult of love up until then. In the sixteenth century, comedies, in which love could play a substantial part, were still few and far between. There was little room for love in tragedies, and in them love was meant to be mocked and derided.

The early years of the seventeenth century saw a shift in emphasis, however, with the proliferation of romanesque and gallant tragedies focusing on figures such as Roland, Médor, Angélique, Bradamante, and Renaud. The Church was determined to stem the tide, and it launched an attack on heterosexual culture as it was portrayed on the stage. For a Church anxious to curb the growing hegemony of heterosexual culture, the theater was a battlefield of choice.

As early as December 1508, the Venetian Consiglio dei Dieci (Council of Ten) issued a decree prohibiting theatrical performances. By the seventeenth century, the theater was under threat in Europe as a whole. In London, Oliver Cromwell imposed a ban that remained in force until after his death in 1658. In Madrid and Paris, theater was also widely condemned. In France, Father Jean Lejeune railed against such worldly pleasures, branding them "incitements to excess."[2] So did celebrated Jansenist theologian Pierre Nicole in his *Traité de la comédie* (Of Comedy):

> The second reason is drawn from the danger of the passion of love, which rules in all comedies.
>
> Our good education bridles this passion and gives it "a certain horror" for us. Comedies and romances, on the other hand, instead of rendering it horrible, make us love it, try to render it honorable. But there is no use in arguing that they deal with honorable passion, for though marriage makes good use of concupiscence, this passion is nevertheless it itself wholly evil and immoderate. . . . We should always regard it as . . . a source of poison.[3]

Not only did the theologians and clerics rise up in arms. Men of letters also joined in the fray. Boileau deplored the "misdeeds and misrepresentations" of the theater and the culture of love and—as was his habit—set out to impose rules and guidelines:

> When, before long, you take your saint to the Opera, how do you think she will look when she casts her eyes on the harmonious pomp of an enchanting spectacle, those dances, those heroes with lustful

voices? She will hear those sonorous speeches about love, those gentle Renauds, those mad Rolands; she will learn from them that one must sacrifice everything, even virtue, to love, as to the one supreme God; that to burn with love too soon is impossible; that heaven has given her a heart only in order to love; and all these commonplaces of lubricious morals will be warmed by the sounds of Lully's music. But when her senses have been stirred this way, what tremors will she feel in her excited heart?[4]

In other words, by the seemingly harmless act of taking his wife to the theater, a man would at once expose her to the risks inherent in music and dance, unchaste enchantment, "harmonious pomp," and, not least, mawkish recitations of love delivered in the seductively mellifluous tones of "those gentle Renauds, those mad Rolands" (Ariosto's token standard-bearers of heterosexual culture). To worship earthly love as if it were "the one supreme God" is, insists Boileau, not only a sin of the flesh but also an affront to the holy spirit, the most grievous sin of all. Lust and lubricity are dangerous enemies that will excite and torture the soul and lead ultimately to perdition.

To condemn bad theater in such scathing terms was one thing, but some means had also to be found to encourage good theater. In France, it was impractical to condemn theater outright, as Cromwell had done in England, since the French monarchy was typically its patron. Caution was indicated if the "base theater of heterosexual love" was to be transformed into "the sublime theater of spiritual grace." As had been already the case with love poetry, it was infinitely preferable to reform as opposed to reject.

There was a considerable body of religious theater in seventeenth-century France, and it was not entirely without merit, although performed chiefly by scholastic institutions and itinerant players touring the provinces. It had, in other words, little or no social cachet or credibility. Paris-based theaters and professional groups of actors had scant place in their repertoire for subject matter they knew would find favor neither with the court nor with the Parisian theatergoing public as a whole.

Around the 1640s or so, however, the situation changed perceptibly, due in no small measure to the influence of Queen Anne of Austria and of various Catholic institutions such as the Company of the Blessed Sacrament created in 1631. Within the space of a few years, all manner of religious drama appeared, including *Saint Eustache* (1638) by Balthasar Baro, *Saul* (1640) and *Esther* (1642) by Pierre Du Ryer, *Sainte Catherine* by Jean Puget de La Serre (1641), *Herménégilde* (1643) by Gautier de Costes (La Calprenède), *Saint Alexis* (1644) and *Le Martyre de saint Genest* (1645) by Nicolas-Marc Desfontaines, and *Le Véritable saint Genest* by Jean Rotrou (1646). In other words, there were signs that religious theater was now capable of competing with the theater of the court.

Beyond any doubt, however, the play that by far best exemplified this new trend was *Polyeucte* by Pierre Corneille. This five-act tragedy based on the life and the martyrdom of Saint Polyeuctus epitomized the opposition between the heterosexual culture of the court and the spiritual demands of the Church. In outline, the plot is comparatively straightforward. At the urging of his friend Nearchus, Polyeuctus (an Armenian nobleman) converts to Christianity against the wishes of his wife, Pauline, and his father-in-law, Felix. The Roman knight Severus, thought to have been killed in battle, has survived and returns to pay court to Pauline, his former lover. Nearchus and Polyeuctus are apprehended after destroying graven images in the Temple of Jupiter. Felix tortures Nearchus in a bid to force Polyeuctus to renounce his Christian faith. The latter refuses and is deaf to the entreaties of Pauline, whom he eventually entrusts to the care of Severus. Polyeuctus is condemned to death, but his exemplary martyrdom persuades Felix and Pauline (and, presumably, Severus) to convert also.

The entire tragedy centers on the juxtaposition of sacred and profane love. At the onset, when Nearchus is at pains to convince Polyeuctus to ignore Pauline's misgivings and have himself baptized without further delay, Polyeuctus initially queries the notion that love of God must take precedence over conjugal love, asking his friend if this Christian God of his is so obdurate and so demanding that loving him means one can love no other. Not so, replies Nearchus:

He suffers us to love all things.
But this our king of kings commands—
That we love and honor him beyond all others
Since there is nought to equal his greatness
And none shall come before or after him.
And to please him we must forsake wife and wealth, rank and state.[5]

Nearchus is adhering to strict and uncompromising Christian orthodoxy when he declares that being a Christian means subordinating love of all things in favor of love of God. "Let feeble women weep," he advises Polyeuctus a few lines earlier. Nearchus, it seems, is not given to sentimentality: he counsels his friend to leave his wife and seek out God— affirming the primacy of the spiritual over the conjugal. In the end, Polyeuctus is convinced, and his new Christian zeal persuades him to destroy the idols in the temple—an act of iconoclasm that is punishable by death. Nearchus tries his to dissuade his friend, but Polyeuctus is fully determined to sacrifice his life in the service of his God:

I shall build him an altar from these idol shards,
For well do I recall your words
That I must love and honor only him,
Forsaking for his dear sake
Wife and wealth and hearth and home.[6]

Here, Polyeuctus throws Nearchus's words back at him, reminding him that "the perfect love" of which he once spoke is not love of the *domina* of *fin'amor* but love of God—that is, not heterosexual but spiritual love. Toward the end of the play, it becomes clear that Pauline's protestations of love and her plaintive tears are no match for Polyeuctus's resolve to embrace martyrdom rather than abjure his new faith. "Your entreaties and your love are as nothing to me," he says bluntly. "I know you not if you are no Christian."[7]

The play does not end there. Polyeuctus is not alone in repudiating profane love. Pauline—at one time in love with Severus (whom she left for Polyeuctus)—also turns her back on earthly love and embraces Christianity. Severus, who has returned expressly to pay court to Pauline, also seems on the verge of converting to Christianity. The tragedy thus ends on a note of collective renunciation of heterosexual love.

The Failure of Religious Drama

In his subsequent *Examen* (exegesis) of *Polyeucte*, Corneille asserted that "the tenderness of human love forms such an agreeable counterpoint to the certainty of divine love that the play has been pleasing to both devout and secular audiences." One ventures to say that Corneille may have been a shade optimistic. According to one reliable source, the play was not received with any great enthusiasm when it was performed at the Hôtel de Rambouillet:

> The play was applauded as a matter of course and in deference to the reputation of its author, but some days later, the poet Vincent Voiture visited Corneille and explained as tactfully as possible that *Polyeucte* had not been the success Corneille assumed it to have been and, in particular, that its Christian overtones had been very poorly received.[8]

This anecdotal evidence is revealing. Voiture evidently bent over backward trying to explain to Corneille that, despite a certain sympathy for the *tendresses de l'amour humain* noted above, the religious elements in the plot had not gone down well with the audience that night at the Hôtel de Rambouillet. The Catholicism of the play was simply unfashionable and certainly not to everyone's taste. In his *Traité de la comédie et des spectacles selon la tradition de l'Église* (1667), the Prince de Conti adopted a broadly similar position, pointing to the fact that the audience had been "a thousand times more receptive to the plight of Severus on discovering that Pauline was married than to the martyrdom of Polyeuctus." A hundred years after that first performance, Voltaire also expressed similar sentiments in the preamble to his own drama *Zaïre*—namely, that the Prince de Conti had correctly adjudged the love interest to be more to the taste of the audience than Corneille's preoccupation with overtly Christian themes.

In effect, the Church's assault on heterosexual culture had failed. Other religious drama dating from around the same time proved equally unsuccessful, although this did not deter Corneille from writing yet another religiously themed play in 1654 (*Théodore, vierge et martyre*), where the saint's repudiation of the flesh and commitment to celibacy forms the nucleus of the plot. Much in the same manner as *Polyeucte*, Corneille's *Théodore* fired yet another broadside in defense of Christian spirituality as superior to heterosexual conjugal love. Despite the author's fame and reputation, however, *Théodore* proved such a resounding failure that Corneille admitted as much in his exegetical commentary to a subsequent comedy titled *La Suite du menteur*, in which he publicly vowed he would never again attempt the same kind of "Christian tragedy." He was true to his word.

In an inquiry into contemporary theater written in 1675 (*Entretien sur les tragédies de son temps*), the Jesuit Abbé de Villiers noted that "following the complete failure of *Théodore*, no one dared write anything similar, that sort of subject matter being confined to instruction in schools." Although Jean Racine did go on to write two *tragédies saintes*, those were written to order and for educational purposes. Religious drama had been discredited and relegated to the halls of academe.

In his tragedies, Corneille attempted to bring out the limits of a culture of love that he claimed must be surpassed, either by reverting to the heroic chivalric values of medieval homosocial culture or in *Polyeucte* and *Théodore* through religion. Audiences had proved increasingly less receptive to his ideas, however, and his reputation declined rapidly as the century progressed. He had been an exceptionally stalwart proponent of chivalric and religious ideals, but he had been unable to hold his own against the burgeoning culture of heterosexual love whose triumph was now complete.

7

The Twentieth Century: The Last Traces of Clerical Opposition

In the eighteenth and nineteenth centuries, the Roman Catholic Church mounted no substantive challenge to the overall legitimacy of heterosexual culture but seemed content to condemn isolated instances of excess. In the absence of a full-scale assault on heterosexuality, the Church identified other priorities, coming out forcefully in opposition to the *philosophes* and the French Revolution in the eighteenth century, for instance, or against the de-Christianization of France in the nineteenth. But an impotent Christian church could only watch helplessly as the fabric of French society was seemingly damaged virtually beyond repair. Up to a point, Catholics suffered in silence, but two pieces of legislation promulgated under the Third Republic persuaded them that they were on the brink of imminent social meltdown.

In 1884, the first of these laws authorized divorce. The sixteenth-century crisis provoked by England's Henry VIII—his petition for divorce, its rejection by Pope Clement VII, the resultant schism between the Church of England and the Roman Catholic Church of Rome, and all the downstream complications that separation had entailed—was still a vivid memory. To many, it was incomprehensible and iniquitous that France—a bastion of the Mother Church—would sanction what was prohibited in canon law. This new piece of legislation might impart autonomy to married life and heterosexual culture and surely infringed on the biblical proscription that "what God hath joined together, let no man put asunder."[1] It now seemed that what God had joined together could indeed be put asunder by the simple expedient of a court order. With a stroke of the pen, the state had encroached on what had traditionally been the Church's prerogative and had undermined a sacrament that had been recognized and respected for over half a millennium.

Even more shocking to Catholic clerics and laymen alike, however, was approval in 1905 of a law providing for the separation of church and state. Suddenly—and almost fifteen hundred years after Clovis, the first king of the Franks, was baptized into the Christian faith—it appeared that the French state was intent on formally renouncing God and repudiating Christianity as the official religion of French public life.

Catholics initially felt traumatized and marginalized in their own country but soon launched an ambitious nationwide program designed to spread the gospel and offset the loss of influence they suffered through this new and, to them, abhorrent law. They invested unprecedented resources in initiatives calculated to mobilize broad-based lay support aimed at reaffirming and strengthening the role of the Church in a changing world.

Although the Church had frequently taken issue with and even condemned the theater, with its back to the wall it was prepared to do whatever seemed necessary to reinforce its position. Many Christians now took the view that the theater could (and should) be acknowledged as a convenient and effective platform from which to reorient this newly secular France. As a result, there was increasing support for a new kind of theater—moralizing and unashamedly Catholic:

A profusion of articles in the Catholic press—contributed not only by journalists but also by theologians, churchmen, academics, and prominent men of letters—called for the moral regeneration of the theater. . . . One objective was to bind the young to the Church in the wake of their first communion, and with that end in mind, the Catholic Church frequently turned to the theater. The output from its *scènes catholiques* may have been at times of dubious quality, but their geographical distribution was impressive: by the 1930s, France boasted around four thousand "theaters" of this kind, regularly playing to large audiences of young and old. Thousands flocked to Passion Plays performed in every part of the country, and youth organizations (e.g., the Christian Workers' Youth Movement and the Union of Young Catholic Agricultural Workers) recruited authors and actors to write and mount genuinely spectacular events, attracting anything up to 100,000 spectators—as was the case at the Parc des Princes in 1937.

. . . Typically, theatrical events of this kind were presided over by the bishops of the diocese in question, and the Church made liberal use of outside performers to celebrate Mass (as in Chartres in 1927, when the theater director, producer, actor, and dramatist Jacques Copeau took a hand in the proceedings). In 1935, 1936, and 1937, the city of Paris mounted a particularly sumptuous *Passion*, a lay production to which the archbishop contributed actors and choirs. Elsewhere, the ceremony of reconsecration of Reims Cathedral (following extensive restoration work completed in 1938) was marked by a mystery play commissioned from the playwright Henri Ghéon and performed by the Compagnons de Jeux in front of the then French president. That same year, Monseigneur Verdier, the successor to His Eminence Cardinal Dubois, became the first prelate ever to set foot inside the Comédie-Française in Paris.[2]

Many Catholic commentators nevertheless continued to regard theater as a major contributory factor to the moral degeneration of France and, more particularly, to the articulation and enactment into law of the 1884 act, inasmuch as the theater had effectively preconditioned audiences to adopt attitudes to divorce that would subsequently be rubber-stamped and legitimized by parliamentary decree. As Pierre Dumaine and others pointed out, "The theater permitted all those who were contemplating divorce to live out their fantasies pending the passage of legal reform."[3] In other words, the theater was held to account for all manner of illicit thoughts and deeds and deemed guilty of explicitly encouraging divorce among many who had perhaps given little thought to the matter before entering the theater. It was felt in many quarters that heterosexual culture, having freed itself from the shackles of religion, had in the process lost all sense of morality and was directly responsible for the morass of spiritual atrophy into which France had sunk.

In practice, innumerable Catholics expressed their dismay that theater—notably the *théâtre de boulevard*—seemed more obsessed than ever with extramarital love, adultery, illicit affairs, and ready recourse to divorce as the sole antidote to a loveless marriage. One commentator (Maurice Brillant) described this as "a poison that must be eliminated,"[4] while another (Charles Dullin, the future head of the Paris-based theater workshop Théâtre de l'Atelier) began encouraging young authors to "depart from the well-trodden path of romanticism with its hackneyed talk of secret trysts and infidelities."[5] Ferdinand-Antonin Vuillermet also wrote of the pernicious effects of the "new morality," which advocated a form of compulsory love and had thereby brought the theater into such disrepute:

> Passion takes precedence over restraint, vice over virtue, the physical over the spiritual; duty has been sacrificed to sensation and goodness is scorned as foolishly naïve. . . . Everything exhibits a brash licentiousness and lewdness unheard of in the theater of thirty or forty years ago.[6]

In attempting to arbitrate between what might be allowed and disallowed in entertainment, Vuillermet concluded that contemporary theater was "preoccupied by pornography" and exhibited an "unhealthy obsession with the unwholesome."[7] In one extreme case in 1929, the Bishop of Arras wrote in his *Lettre pastorale* that the theater, by reason of its insistent advocacy of indiscriminate heterosexual love, had been directly responsible for a specific case of *crime passionel* in his diocese.

Catholics were far from alone in their criticism of this new permissiveness. Gustave Lanson, the director of the prestigious *École normale supérieure*, was someone else who found the "new metaphysic of love" to be "somewhat distasteful,"[8] and in his autobiography (*Un régulier dans le siècle*, A Plain Man of His Time), French philosopher and novelist Julien Benda noted that the plays of Georges de Porto-Riche, one of the most popular boulevard playwrights of the age, were "disturbingly love-oriented," "low and distasteful," and "replete with all the posturing braggadocio of the enlisted man."[9]

On the eve of World War I, comments such as the above were even more significant in the light of growing concerns that the birth rate in

France had fallen to such dangerously low levels that the country might be unable to defend itself in times of war. Such fears were related to the new notions of love that swept the country as a whole and the capital in particular. A number of commentators remarked on the correlation between France's falling birth rate and the popularity of theater. Cardinal Dubois specifically noted that "the theater must shoulder a large part of the responsibility for the current decline in our country's population."[10] In one of his circulars, he singled out for the severest criticism what he termed "the theater of immorality, lewdness, and crime" that had contributed to a society that was "intensely self-centered and intent only on pleasure to the detriment of the soul."[11]

Some criticisms were even more blunt. In 1924, an issue of the thrice-yearly *Bulletin* of the Bordeaux Council for the Protection of the Moral Welfare of the Young and the Suppression of Public License and Disorder condemned "immoral enterprises that threaten our country with sterility and place us in a delicate and perilous situation in relation to other countries."[12] Abbé Bethléem, who had been very active in Christian theater, remarked that "the theater in France talks incessantly of love but makes little mention of children, as if there were no correlation whatsoever between the two."[13] This was an opinion shared by many in the Church, who frequently recorded their misgivings that heterosexual couples had been accorded such a degree of autonomy that they had acquired unprecedented moral and religious freedom and had also been absolved of any obligation to "be fruitful and multiply." It appeared that the theater had spawned a culture of love for love's sake.

Around 1920, there were fresh calls to relaunch the antipornography campaigns of yesteryear that had targeted billboard and poster advertising that were found to be obscene. A number of prominent citizens were involved in the ensuing crusades, including General de Castelnau, Field Marshal Ferdinand Foch, and the wife of General Weygand. The National Federation of Catholics—whose membership grew to some 700,000—played an important role in campaigns directed against pornography, the perfidious influence of the theater, contraception, and abortion. The Church was making every effort to bring married couples within the ambit of its various initiatives at a juncture when cheap theater and pornography tended to regard physical love (and contraception) as an end in itself.

Antipornography campaigns targeted the theater, *café concerts*, and the music halls and attempted to involve local mayoral offices and departmental prefectures. Censorship had been repealed by a decree law of 1906,[14] but recourse could still be had to article 28 of the decree law dated July 29, 1881, which specifically (and conveniently) prohibited "material prejudicial to good morals" and could, for example, be applied to obscenities uttered on stage or even be used to forestall any performance deemed potentially licentious. The Third National Congress against Pornography held in March 1922 debated how best to tackle the issue. A precedent of sorts had been hinted at in an item in the *Revue pénitentiaire* (Prison Gazette) of 1912, which stipulated that

> A mayor shall have the right to review a written copy of any play and to accept or reject it as he deems appropriate. He shall at all times be entitled to attend or be represented at a public performance, and should the author(s) alter or expand the text by means of word, gesture, or intimation, he shall have the right to intervene and call the proceedings to a halt.[15]

Various parliamentarians now called for legislation aimed at curbing potential abuses in the theater, and several mayors and prefects expressed agreement with provisions designed to censor or at least mitigate bad theater. René Wisner, a dramatist, came out strongly against productions that were "consistently unfaithful to the original text and concerned only to pander to an audience's baser instincts."[16] Specific plays were subjected to close scrutiny. Thus, a performance of Racine's *Phaedra* in Lorraine was canceled on the grounds that it "might give children the wrong idea."[17] The operetta *Le Truc de Micheline* was also blocked (one suspects on the strength of the suggestive *truc* alone). The citizens of one commune were so zealous that they proposed changing the title of the celebrated and immensely popular play *The Game of Love and Chance* written by Pierre de Marivaux nearly two centuries previously.

It was also pointed out that the fires of courage and self-sacrifice rekindled by the Great War had long since been extinguished. Paul Reynaud did not mince words when he asked, "What did you all expect? That the Great War would perhaps get us out of the cesspit we're in?"[18]

And he had this to say to the *poilus* (other ranks) who put pleasure before moralizing: "Then open the floodgates and let the crap flow in!"[19] Other comments were less graphic:

Victory will be conditional on sustaining the purity and moral and physical resilience of the French soldier. There must be no question of humoring him in the form of cheap vaudevillian farce replete with cuckolded husbands, jilted lovers, jaded mistresses, feral couplings, and other lurid and thoroughly unedifying matters.[20]

The perceived need was therefore to separate the wheat from the chaff—to weed out the unwanted excesses of deregulated heterosexuality while preserving both the virtues implicit in Christianity and a sense of the heroic as exemplified in wartime. In this respect, as in many others, the twentieth-century anti-Eros debate appeared to reprise allegations not dissimilar to those once leveled against thirteenth-century love poetry, sixteenth-century *Amours*, and seventeenth-century court theater—that heterosexual culture had proved conducive to diminished virility (a gender issue) and that preoccupation with love had been at the expense of procreation (a sex issue). There were fears that the problem was getting out of hand in the post–World War I context where sexual pleasure seemed increasingly to take precedence over (Christian) self-sacrifice, *virtus*, and duty.

There were other complications, not least the progressively crude manner in which heterosexual love was frequently portrayed. In the days of Racine, Marivaux, and Beaumarchais, declarations of love had at least donned the cloak of linguistic respectability. Not so in the twentieth century, when love was increasingly presented in terms that commentators described as vulgar, crude, base, and obscene, devoid of class in any sense of the word. In Paris, peripheral boulevard theater attracted a new audience whose sensibilities and behavior were at odds with the upper-class and aristocratic core values projected by the Comédie-Française. Boulevard theatergoers were drawn from the hoi polloi, and the downmarket entertainment served up to them was anathema to upmarket theater critics writing in *Le Figaro* or *La Croix*. The vocabulary they used in their reviews showed that the problem was now a question of not only sex and gender but also class.

It was one thing to complain about bad theater but another entirely to set about improving it. What kinds of plays were desirable? And more to the point, what needed to be done to foster a Catholic repertoire worthy of the name?

Whereas it was relatively simple to identify individual anti-Catholic plays in terms of subject matter and tone, it proved substantially more difficult to build a coherent Catholic repertoire. A roster of Catholic playwrights nonetheless resolved to focus on subjects other than sex, infidelity, adultery, and the like. Among them were Henri Ghéon, Jacques Debout, Gabriel Marcel, René des Granges, Alice Rolland, Henri Cochard, Jeanne Leroy-Denis, Marguerite Perroy, Adrienne Blanc-Péridier, Marguerite Duportal, and Henriette Charasson. For the most part, their focus was on the antithesis between human and divine love and on the reconciliation of the sacred and the secular.

Yet another name to be added to this distinguished list is that of the maverick—but incontestably Catholic—author and dramatist Paul Claudel. In his autobiographical *Break of Noon*, Claudel also explores what, for him, was a "self-evident antithesis." On the face of it, the illicit and passionate encounter between Ysé de Ciz and her Chinese lover, Mesa, is—as Claudel stressed—"utterly banal," but it provides a convenient backdrop for his inquiry into the nature of adultery and "the conflict between spiritual love and the pleasures of the flesh." François Mauriac later expressed delight at how successfully Claudel had "introduced a spiritual dimension into a vaudevillian setting" to the extent that he had managed to impart "a presence stronger than the Fate of Greek tragedy at the epicenter of the play, which turns from a tale of carnal pleasure into a drama of divine grace."

Claudel reprised the theme in his last and best-known play, *The Tidings Brought to Mary*, a dramatized meditation on the incarnation (that is, the word made flesh), which juxtaposes two sisters (Mara and Violaine) who represent carnal and spiritual love, respectively. *Break of Noon* and *The Tidings Brought to Mary* are potent demonstrations of Claudel's preoccupation with the superiority of the love of God and are significant contributions to the manner in which the notion of love was explored and revised in Catholic theater.

Henri Ghéon, although largely forgotten today, was a leading light in Christian theater at the turn of the twentieth century. Ghéon—a founding member of and contributor to the illustrious *Nouvelle Revue Française* and a close friend and confidant of fellow homosexual André Gide—was a lapsed and subsequently born-again Catholic who devoted his entire literary output to the glorification of God. Ghéon was a prominent man of letters, and Catholic hopes vested in him as the potential spearhead of theatrical reform and the elaboration of a new repertoire. Ghéon authored an impressive number of plays with religious themes and was celebrated in his day as the model Catholic playwright. One of Ghéon's plays that was selected to be performed during the 1938 inauguration of the newly restored Reims Cathedral. Although he was respected and admired by the Catholic community, Ghéon never quite succeeded in making his presence felt beyond it. André Gide once cautioned him that "good intentions don't make for good literature," a cruel remark relished and repeated in Parisian literary circles. Maurice Brillant, an active proponent of the genre, also went on record in 1922 to the effect that "boredom is the single greatest enemy of Christian theater." The remark was not directed toward Ghéon, but it indicates the uphill task that faced any dramatist who wrote in this narrow form.

The high point of Ghéon's career—and possibly of Christian theater generally—was widely expected to be achieved when his *The Poor Man under the Stairs* was first performed in public on January 24, 1921, at Jacques Copeau's prestigious Théâtre du Vieux-Colombier in Paris. It was a momentous occasion—a Christian play in Copeau's experimental theater workshop with none other than Copeau himself in the title role. Catholic theater appeared to have come of age with a vengeance and to have emerged at last from the obscurity to which it had been consigned since the days of Corneille.

The plot is familiar from the eleventh-century *Life of Saint Alexis* discussed earlier, which recounts the life of the eponymous saint who leaves his bride and sets off on his travels in search of God. He returns home many years later and, instead of making himself known to his wife and parents, hides out under the stairs and dies destitute. The message is unequivocal: love of God transcends all earthly love. This is in the tradition of Christian orthodoxy as embraced by theologians and clerics from Saint

Paul to Saint Pierre Damian by way of Saint Thomas and Saint Jerome. Heterosexuality is not to be dismissed out of hand, but marriage and married life are nothing compared with divine love, the primacy of which was repeatedly proclaimed all the way from the *ur*-text of the *Life of Saint Alexis* to Corneille's *Polyeucte*. In his bid to postulate a viable Catholic alternative to boulevard theater, it seemed that Henri Ghéon could not have chosen a more appropriate theme.

The play was a flop. Many devout Catholics—married and with large families to support—were unable to empathize with the poor man of the title, saint or otherwise, as pointed out by Ghéon himself in a preface to the work:

> As soon as it is presented as an example, the exceptional case of Alexis seems to us to run counter to the values of society, family, and marriage. What is to be gained by his example? He may be a superhuman; he may also no longer be human. Behind your mask of Catholicism, you are, like the others, a mere artist and entertainer at heart.

The fact was that even a predominantly Catholic audience failed to see what Ghéon—and, by extension, the Church—hoped to achieve by all this talk of *amour céleste* as opposed to *amour terrestre*. Heterosexual culture had by this time become so second nature to and so ingrained in contemporary Christian ethic that the public at large was not prepared to admit any derogation from it, irrespective of anything and everything saints and theologians of the past might have said. The public was unwilling to recognize "the poor man under the stairs" as anything other than "nonhuman" and, in consequence, "unnatural." Ghéon's decidedly lame explanation did little to convince the audience otherwise. *The Poor Man under the Stairs*—one of the most costly failures both in Copeau's career and in the long and distinguished history of the Vieux-Colombier—was axed from the company's repertoire on short notice.

Amazingly, an unrepentant Ghéon planned to offer Copeau and the Vieux-Colombier a second religious play, titled *The Three Miracles of Saint Cecilia*. The first act features a couple of Roman newlyweds (Cecilia and Valerian), the second focuses on the martyrdom of the latter, while the third and final act explores the martyrdom of Cecilia. Once again, sacred and profane loves are juxtaposed. The play opens on the protagonists' wedding night, with the new bride modestly but firmly warding off the advances of her patrician husband, explaining to his astonishment that she is already married and cannot give herself to another, not even her lawfully wedded husband: "Christ is my Lord, and I became his bride from the morning I first heard his name. / Our nuptials, dear friend, shall be no impediment for he shall celebrate them in his mansion." Understandably perhaps, Valerian is beside himself with frustration ("And this is how our wedding night shall end? . . . Oh, empty night! All passion dead / And never known"). Ultimately, however, Valerian enters a state of grace and also converts to Christianity. To a degree, *The Three Miracles* carries on from where *The Poor Man under the Stairs* left off. Cecilia's subsequent martyrdom is both suitably epic and heroically Christian in scale, and her rejection of heterosexual love in favor of love of God is suitably dramatic.

Sadly for Ghéon, however, Jacques Copeau was (understandably) reluctant to embark on a second project that had all the hallmarks of the first and turned down *The Three Miracles*. The play was destined never to see the light of day at the Vieux-Colombier. And it brought down the final curtain on Christian theater in the nation's capital, consigning the genre to provincial playhouses and church halls.

A number of other plays written around this time took up the theme of physical versus spiritual love, including *Le Monde cassé* (The Broken World) by Gabriel Marcel or *Marie de la Chapelle* by Jacques Debout. But optimistic Catholic campaigns to clean up vaudeville and boulevard theater and banish the cult of adultery from Parisian stages were already dead in the water. None of the exponents of this particular theatrical genre succeeded in making his mark with the contemporary public at large or posterity. Ghéon is perhaps not entirely forgotten although even an informed literary public will have considerable difficulty in naming anything by him. As for others of his ilk who were once household names in Catholic theater (Brochet, Debout, Domaine, and so on), little trace now remains. Gabriel Marcel is remembered by some but as a philosopher rather than as a relatively prolific author of religious drama. The only religious dramatist to have stood the test of time is Paul Claudel (who, significantly perhaps, was never formally identified with the movement).

Despite being condemned by the Church, boulevard theater is alive and well to this day, and the subject of adultery and illicit love is a theatrical staple and the mainstay of countless films and television programs. The wide-ranging and sustained attack on heterosexual culture essayed by Christian society had proved a resounding failure.

PART III

Medical Opposition to Heterosexual Culture

The Roman Catholic Church and the nobility were not alone in their opposition to the cult of heterosexual love, which had grown more popular in the final third of the Middle Ages before emerging as a major cultural paradigm in the sixteenth century. Those in the medical profession had also opposed it, believing that undue preoccupation with love and passion were a sociopathological condition and symptomatic of an epidemic that they were duty-bound to address. It was in this context that the theory of lovesickness evolved. The notion actually dated from antiquity—exemplified *inter alia* by Ovid's *Remedia amoris* (The Cure for Love)—but was nearly forgotten until it resurfaced at the close of the Middle Ages.

8

Heterosexual Love and Medieval and Renaissance Medicine

Love and leprosy were so closely associated in the medieval mind that it was frequently asserted that the peasant underclass typically contracted the disease (among others) as a result of excessive sexual activity. Jacques Le Goff quotes from a sermon delivered by Caesarius of Arles in the first half of the sixth century in which the bishop cautions his flock against sexual incontinence on the grounds that it may result in leprous, epileptic, or even demonic offspring.[1] Accordingly—and not least since spiritual and physical well-being were held to be analogous—love and the pleasures of the flesh were regarded as unsavory practices from both religious and medical perspectives.

This medical insight is mentioned in various medieval discourses on the subject, notably in one by Andreas Capellanus, who employed it to condemn love and lovers on the grounds that the act of copulation ("the work of Venus") weakens the body and diminishes a man's prowess in battle. This occurs, he explained, "for three reasons well-known to physicians": first, the physical act sapped vital energies; second, it blunted the appetite so that men ate and drank less and became weaker; and third, it deprived men of rest and sleep, damaging the digestive system and causing a major loss of physical strength.[2] Thus, over and above moral and spiritual objections to the physical act, insisted Capellanus, there were also compelling medical reasons in support of his argument.

An Inflammation of Blood and Liver

In the Renaissance and the seventeenth century, it was generally accepted that love was a particularly insidious condition that the medical profession needed to describe and address—a "pathology of love" that resulted from the emergent heterosexual culture and that, despite everything, was steadily infiltrating contemporary literature and society. The profession's attitudes in this respect did not reveal any radical departure from those that were held in the Middle Ages and in antiquity, but in line with Renaissance practice, their exposition was now more systematic.

Two individual discourses stand out in this context—*L'Antidote d'amour*[3] by Jean Aubéry and *De la maladie d'amour ou melancholie erotique* by Jacques Ferrand. In his author's preface to the former, Aubéry defended himself against the potential charge of underlying prejudice in his work, insisting that he should on no account be considered emasculated ("Some . . . might think me a eunuch of sorts escaped from the harem"). This is a significant disclaimer in that it reveals the extent to which many of his contemporaries regarded physical love as an integral component of virility. For a medical man such as himself, on the other hand, it was love itself that emasculates, real men being those who succeeded in resisting temptation. This was essentially a gender issue: should masculinity be defined in terms of the cult of love or by its refusal? Jean Aubéry doubtless knew this was still a matter for debate, although he had come down on the side of the latter option. For all that, he stressed that he himself had "experienced" physical love on several occasions, thereby going some way toward reassuring his readership that he was no eunuch.

Like Hippocrates bent on ridding Athens of the plague, Aubéry was committed to banishing physical love from the world in the interest of restoring spiritual freedom. As a physician, he considered it his duty to explore and teach methods by which the soul was to be liberated from the tyranny of the body and its ailments and afflictions. Inasmuch as Socratic tradition consistently held that the physician was to the body what the philosopher was to the soul, there was a clear philosophical duality at work here. This is implicit in the second chapter of *L'Antidote d'amour*, which asserts that man is not intrinsically and necessarily made for physical love. Quite the contrary: to love or not to love is a decision each individual is at liberty to make: "God has given man freedom of choice," noted Aubéry.

Aubéry's position is not readily reconciled. After all, if love is an illness, how can it be a matter of choice? The etiology of love is problematic: it is either an illness or an act of free will. It cannot be both. The contradiction, however, was only apparent. The love that Aubéry had in mind was comparable to other pathogens, such as, say, alcohol. The consumption of alcohol may be a matter for individual choice, but it can also lead to serious illness and become itself a pathological condition known as alcoholism. With love as with alcohol, yielding to one's bodily desires meant renouncing rationality; there was a direct link between the care of the body and the care of the soul, between free will and pathology.

Aubéry could not escape the requirement that he define the causes and nature of love for the purposes of his argument. He distinguished two specific variants: "There are two loves, one celestial and virtuous, the other sensual or voluptuous, the former housed in the temperate mind, the latter in the liver." Clearly, the former (good) love drew heavily on "celestial and virtuous" precepts of the Christian ethos and morality, whereas the latter (bad) love was rooted not in the mind but in another organ entirely. The difference between the two was thus fundamental and substantive rather than one merely of degree. According to Aubéry, this second kind of love had once debased Hercules, brought about the fall of Troy, and been the ruin of Antony and Cleopatra. This interpretation is in line with sentiments expressed in heroic Renaissance tragedies authored by writers like Étienne Jodelle and Robert Garnier.

Taken as a whole, the antilove strictures voiced by physicians generally were influenced by both religious and chivalric traditions. The stance of the medical profession was both a matter of *sex* (as it was for the Church, which is why Aubéry privileged a love that was "celestial and virtuous") and a matter of *gender* (as it was for warriors, which is why he condemned the "sensual or voluptuous" love that had rendered base and effeminate heroes such as Hercules, Mark Antony, and many others).

As a physician, Aubéry was primarily preoccupied with the second kind of love, where some sort of medical intervention was indicated. To postulate a "physiology of love," he looked to the body rather than to the soul. Accordingly, he went on to define lovesickness, stating that body temperature will rise if a patient is exposed to an object of beauty but that when body temperature increases above a certain point, the patient will fall ill. The locus or seat of the disorder was neither in the head nor in the stomach but in the liver (the organ he described as "the material cause of love"), and when an individual was afflicted by love, his blood would literally boil:

Instead of an eagle a cruel obsession
Soiling its claw in my eternal wound
Gnaws my liver.

The quotation is from *Les Amours*, in which Pierre de Ronsard often alludes to the myth of Prometheus tortured by an eagle clawing at his exposed liver, the implication being that the "agony of love" endured by the poet is on a par with the suffering to which Prometheus was subjected. Whereas a modern reader would take this to be little more than a metaphor drawn from mythology, Aubéry uses the verse to go further, accepting the image not only mythologically but also physiologically. The eagle tearing at Prometheus's liver lays bare the burning wound of an organ infected by the disease of love. Aubéry seems to be suggesting that, while Ronsard may not have been aware of the specific nature and cause of the disorder, he nevertheless recognized it and sourced it intuitively to the correct organ of the body. To put it another way, the modern reader approaches the text as literature, whereas Aubéry reads it as an exercise in medical hermeneutics.

L'Antidote d'amour is replete with such allusions and quotations, frequently from Ronsard, which is unsurprising, given that the physicians of the age were determined to address the pathology caused by poetry written in praise of heterosexual love. Accordingly, Aubéry constantly referred to those deemed responsible for the phenomenon, among them the pairings of Virgil and Alexis,[4] Catullus and Lesbia, Tibullus and Nemesis, Ovid and Corinna, Petrarch and Laura, and, most of all perhaps, Ronsard and Cassandra. These and others like them had contributed decisively to the culture of love poetry, which had now spread like an "epidemic" that Aubéry and physicians like him were resolved to treat and, where possible, eradicate.

As to precisely how this mysterious "boiling of the blood" came about, Aubéry asserts in chapter 3 of his treatise that "it is the senses that deliver our soul to passion." The soul may be perfect, he explained, but it is deceived and betrayed by the senses, which transmit all manner of false information, in much the same way as a prince might be deluded into poor decisions on the basis of inaccurate reports from one of his courtiers. Aubéry argued that the sense of sight was particularly relevant, since it stimulated desire: the eyes of a beautiful woman sent out "rays" that were received by a prospective lover and that literally caused the latter's temperature to rise. By way of illustration, Aubéry quoted Ronsard again and interpreted his lines to arrive at a preconceived medical diagnosis. The woman's eyes in Ronsard's sonnets send out rays like metaphorical arrows loosed from Cupid's bow, but Aubéry took this metaphor literally, insisting that such rays warmed the blood, which, carried via the nerves to the liver, then turned into bile and gave off "evil humors." This inflammation of the blood and liver was, he insisted, the root cause of "lovesickness." As for the other senses, they too could stimulate physical desire (admittedly to a lesser extent). Aubéry was convinced, for example, that the ears were susceptible in much the same way as the eyes inasmuch as many prospective suitors were aroused—sight unseen—by descriptions of a potential loved one and vivid tales of her alleged perfections. The sense of smell could also prove a deleterious stimulant, as indeed could that of touch, to the extent that certain odors and certain forms of caress had aphrodisiacal properties. The sense of sight, however, remained the most common source of love.

Love could also be influenced by specific circumstances and individual factors. Age was a case in point, since it was generally accepted that the young and those in their prime were the most ardent lovers (as opposed to children and the aged). The reason, Aubéry submitted, was self-evident: the blood of the elderly already ran cold, and that of children had yet to heat up enough. Gender was also a factor, he added, inasmuch as the female, though colder than the male, was also weaker, and therefore the effects of her heat were to be expected sooner. This also explained why young girls were more precocious as far as puberty was concerned: they were less able than their male counterparts to resist passion.

Other factors heightened the risk of falling victim to the *maladie d'amour*. Those who were by nature of "hot and humid blood" were, for example, more disposed to love. Meanwhile, "the bilious are more prompt and ardent but less capable of moderation, their temperament as hot and dry as sulfur or a dry twig that can readily burst into flame" but will burn only for a very short time. Not least, "phlegmatics and melancholics were more knowing in their choice of love partners," given that their colder blood did not lend itself to spontaneity and tended to make them less passionate and more calculating.

Nor did it end there. Account had yet to be taken of the complex matter of seasonal variation. After the chill of winter, said Aubéry, spring was the most propitious season for love (Ronsard, for one, would have agreed with him, although Aubéry does not trouble to quote him in this instance).[5] For some, however, winter would actually be the more propitious, since the major body organs—the liver especially—generated and stored more heat to offset and banish the chill of winter. And what of summer? Shouldn't summer be the season of love? Perhaps not, said Aubéry, since people appeared too languid and listless and "more in need of cooling refreshment to temper their ardor."

Aubéry also addressed at length the possibility that love could be induced by ingesting love potions, as in the celebrated case of Tristan and Iseult. This prompted him to inquire whether love might not be *causa sui*—that is, self-generating and sufficient unto itself ("Is love the cause of love?"). Aubéry couldn't help but notice how "easy" love was.

Following protracted discussion of the possible causes of love, Aubéry then turns his attention to its effects. Among other things, he points out, it weakens the body and slows the pulse rate. Those who are "love-sick" often tend to lose weight since they are too distracted to remember to eat and even when they do take nourishment, they fail to digest it properly since all the heat necessary to the digestive process is concentrated in the liver.

Sighing was seen as another classic symptom of lovesickness. Dreaming of one's love (so the theory went) clouds the mind and causes the lovelorn momentarily to forget to breathe. Deprived of air, the body compensates by inhaling rapidly and often, causing the patient to sigh. Didn't Ronsard once complain of "a thousand thousand sighs" that caused his sides to ache? And was it not significant that the word *suitor* is sometimes rendered in French by *soupirant* (literally, "sighing")?

Insomnia was another symptom singled out by Aubéry. Sleep, he points out, is induced by a "vapor" known as *anathimiasis*, which is produced by a gastric condition where the patient is listless and sluggish (typically after a copious meal). However, since the lovelorn rarely take the trouble to eat and were known to digest poorly anything they did eat, they generate next to no *anathimiasis* and, as a result, sleep poorly (if at all). Not least, *L'Antidote d'amour* points to the revealing fact that the hands and other extremities of those suffering from lovesickness are typically cold. This, we learn, is because the hot blood retreats to the center of the body and concentrates itself in the liver.

The physicians of the day appeared well served in terms of diagnostic options, such as insomnia, suspiration, weight loss, diminished heart rate, and so on. The big question is whether the treatment they subsequently prescribed proved successful. In the closing pages of his discourse, Aubéry listed a certain number of remedies and therapies that he had applied to great effect. Those who suspect they may be suffering from lovesickness should refer to Jean Aubéry's recommendations or consult their own family doctor.

Erotic Melancholy and Feminine Hysteria

A treatise by Jacques Ferrand[6] offers a further representative example of the hostility that the medical profession reserved for the culture of heterosexuality. In a preface to the work, Ferrand cites diverse authorities, including the Persian polymath and physician Avicenna, the medieval theorist Bernard of Gordon, the Florentine Marsilio Ficino, and the French naturalist and physician Guillaume Rondelet. He then takes to task those who deny that love is an illness and who spend their days devising ways to praise what is, ultimately, the root cause of their indisposition. Like Jean Aubéry, Ferrand is adamant that the poets are to blame for this insidious illness they insist on celebrating. Anticipating a charge that psychoanalysis would also face some centuries later, Ferrand also takes issue with what he regards as bad faith on the part of his patients.

In essence, Ferrand shares Aubéry's views on lovesickness, not least to the extent that he also ascribes the condition to an "overheating" of the blood that can give rise to some rather surprising symptoms. He notes that "Phaëtusa, who loved Pytheus her husband dearly but who was not able to enjoy him due to his long absence, therewith became a man with body hair, a masculine voice, and a beard." Ferrand is in no way surprised by what at first glance appears to be a rather strange phenomenon since, for him, the difference between men and women lies principally in the sexual organs, which, in the women's case, are simply retained inside the body for lack of heat, as both Aristotle and Galen had pointed out. However a women "on heat" could eventually take on the secondary sexual characteristics of a man. That being so, he argued, Renaissance love culture, with its emphasis on passion and eroticism, might well have the effect of making men more effeminate and women more masculine. What Ferrand was saying, in so many words, was that heterosexual culture was a threat to the separation and differentiation of the sexes.

Ferrand enumerated factors that increased the risks of *innamoramento* (falling in love). Over and above those listed by Aubéry, he added climatic and regional factors. To the extent that passion was "heat-related," it was understandable that those living in northern climes should be less susceptible to the disease of love than "the Egyptians, Arabians, Moors, and Spanish," who were notoriously prone to passion. Ferrand also pointed to heredity as a contributory factor and risk: a man whose father had been profligate would exhibit a similar tendency, always assuming his personality was not tempered by education and an appropriately administered health *régime*.

Two main concepts set Ferrand's treatise apart from that of Aubéry, and the first of these is his notion of "erotic melancholy" or "erotomania." In the Renaissance, melancholy was often associated with Saturn, but in this instance, the emphasis is strictly on the organic as opposed to the astrological. To use Ferrand's own words, erotic *melancholia* is perhaps best described as a "form of insanity arising from an inordinate desire to enjoy an object of beauty, an insanity accompanied by intense fear and sadness." Melancholy—as the original Greek implies—is attributable to a surfeit of black bile and characterized by irascibility, depression, and an inability to think clearly.

Love, in other words, confuses and obfuscates. This, argued Ferrand, is what is meant when love is characterized as "blind"—not because Cupid is literally blindfolded but because the black bile of erotic melancholy persuades young lovers that the grotesquely ugly partner to whom they are drawn is—notwithstanding her "craggy brow, thick tufted eyebrows, weepy eyes, pendulous ears, . . . squashed nose, big blubbery lips curled inwards, teeth black and stinking" and "protuberant chin twisted into a hideous frown"—actually a woman of singular beauty ("a second Helen"), with a smooth and alabaster-like forehead, ebony-black eyebows, and gentle and pellucid eyes that radiate love and promises of happiness. Ferrand's broadside of bravura satire was directly inspired by sixteenth-century *contr'amours* (declamatory satirical antilove verse) authored by writers like Du Bellay, Jodelle, Tahureau, and Platina.[7] In a few short lines, Ferrand succinctly encapsulates and satirizes the extent to which lovers were at the mercy of poets whose imagination and invention were, to his mind, ludicrously replete with banal Petrarchan cliché and overworked *canzoniere* metaphor ("alabaster-like forehead," "eyes like stars," "ebony-black eyebows," and so on).

The second concept introduced by Ferrand was that of hysteria. When a woman fell in love, he explained, she produced seed that, if not used, tended to accumulate in the womb, where it degraded and provoked severe itching. He went on to point out that "hysterical women" have a compulsive need to speak (not least about sex), since self-expression helps mitigate the discomfort and itching they feel in their womb. Hysteria is thus another form of erotic melancholy.

Ferrand's argument drew on widely circulated ideas about the uterus. Paracelsus had asserted that every female ailment could be sourced to the womb, a view largely shared by François Mauriceaux, the leading obstetrician of his day in France, who was fully prepared to attribute "the majority" of female ailments to it. A woman's whole life appeared to be dominated by this capriciously autonomous little animal called the uterus (Greek: *hystera*), of which the celebrated court physician Jean Fernel once wrote: "When irritated and angered, it withdraws from its proper place and moves elsewhere to escape what is foreign and hostile and search out what is gentle and pleasing."[8] To contemporary theorists as a whole, hysteria was a condition directly brought on by "constriction and suffocation of the womb" or by *furor uteri*, where "seed" and menstrual blood putrified in the womb, decomposing and giving off a toxic vapor capable of infecting the entire body, including the brain.

As a general rule, the uterus was coveted by men. Plato stated as much in his *Timaeus*,[9] and Rabelais made the same point in his *Tiers Livre*.[10] This provoked considerable confusion in matters of love, to the point where numerous physicians counseled strict abstinence or out-and-out celibacy in an effort to curb excesses generated by the now fashionable culture of heterosexuality. For this reason, expertise in questions pertaining to love and marriage was seen to be the prerogative of medicine. In a sense, physicians now exerted authority not only over their own patients: their bedside manner, it seemed, was applicable to society as a whole.

The Seventeenth Century: From Lovesickness to Curative Love

The antieroticism that was once universally advocated in certain medical circles was progressively offset by currents of philoeroticism in others. Whereas physicians such as Aubéry and Ferrand looked on love as an affliction, others saw it as a potential remedy. When a woman was "sick with love," a growing number of physicians had, as early as the sixteenth century, already started recommending heterosexual intercourse as a potential cure.

In *La Curiosité naturelle*, Scipion Dupleix argued that as soon as a young woman started to look wan and out of sorts, it was high time her parents thought about marrying her off. Elsewhere, the renowned court surgeon Ambroise Paré recommended much the same thing, albeit in somewhat cruder terms. When a married woman fell ill, he advised, the best remedy of all was a good "seeing-to" by her husband. In his *Livre de la nature et utilité des moys des femmes et de la curation des maladies qui en surviennent*, anatomist Jacques Sylvius addressed the issue of menstruation and related problems, remarking *inter alia* that if a nun, widow, celibate woman, or "one neglected by her husband" were deprived of physical congress, then rather than produce an embryo, she would run the risk that the "fluid" she secreted would accumulate in the womb, rot, and cause hysteria. Playing the "love game" (for it was not only a matter of sex) was considered conducive to good health. As Ambroise Paré pointed out, if a woman was not *amoureuse*, her fluid would not be sufficiently warmed, and intercourse would be sterile and unproductive; worse, she was liable to abort (a compelling reason for not forcing young women to marry against their will).

Heterosexual culture was now in the process of being endorsed by the medical profession.

Love as a Remedy

When advanced by Renaissance physicians, the notion of love as a palliative seemed bold and decidedly avant-garde. By the seventeenth century, however, it had become commonplace, so much so that the pros and cons were openly debated even outside medical circles, not least in the theater in farces, for example, and in the comedies of Molière. In his early one-act farce *Le Médecin volant*, for instance, Valère loves Lucile, but her father Gorgibus is against their union. Lucile pretends to be ill, and Valère's valet Sganarelle disguises himself as the eponymous "flying doctor." In scene 3, Gros-René criticizes his master Gorgibus's attitude to Lucile:

> What the deuce are you thinking about, intending to give your daughter in marriage to some old man? Isn't it obvious that it is the love she bears for the young one that is making her ill?

Gros-René may be a simple peasant (as his name is intended to suggest), but he has hit on the right diagnosis. All the signs point to Lucile as being in the throes of erotic melancholy. Granted, her illness may be feigned, but the sadness provoked by her father's reluctance to let her see her beloved Valère is most certainly genuine. Pretense has become reality.

Mention might also be made of Molière's *Le Médecin malgré lui*, which hinges on a similar plot. This time, it is Lucinde who is in love with Léandre, whose father is opposed to their union. Lucinde pretends to be mute, and Sganarelle—Léandre's accomplice—dresses up as a doctor and pretends he can cure her. Jacqueline, a nurse, has her own ideas:

> Believe me, the best medicine one could ever give your daughter would be a handsome strapping husband for her to love. Let me tell you and a dozen like you, that all the doctors in the world will do her

no good at all. What she needs is something else. And a husband is a plaster that will cure any girl's complaints.

In these two excerpts, lovesickness is promptly and accurately diagnosed by a valet and a nurse, a clear indication that the condition is recognized at all levels of society. According to both Gros-René and Jacqueline, the most effective remedy for lovesickness is love itself.

Yet another Molière play addresses the same theme (which was evidently dear to the playwright's heart): in *L'Amour médecin*—in essence, a reprise of *Le Médecin volant*—it is the turn of Sganerelle's daughter to affect melancholia. Her father falls for the ruse:

Ah, there goes my daughter, taking the air. She does not see me. She sighs and lifts her eyes to the heavens. And she is so sad and melancholic.

The sighs and the melancholia are by now classic symptoms of lovesickness, as recognized by Jean Aubéry and Jacques Ferrand. Various doctors are consulted, and each presents his antilove diagnosis. Their deliberations are mercilessly parodied:

Dr. Tomes: Sir, we have consulted in the matter of your daughter's illness, and it is my conclusion that she suffers from a severe overheating of the blood and must be bled as soon as possible.

Dr. Fonandres: In my opinion, her illness is caused by an infection due to a surfeit of humors. I advise that she be given an emetic.

Dr. Bahys: Inasmuch as these humors have been present for a long time, they have reheated and engendered a malignity whose fumes rise toward the brain.

Needless to say, none of the above succeeds in effecting a cure. Clitandre then arrives on the scene, claiming to be a physician. The young man is in reality the object of the girl's affection, whose suit has, to her dismay, been rejected by her father. Clitandre confirms that the girl is indeed mad, that she wishes to wed, and that the only solution would seem to be to conduct a bogus wedding ceremony to placate her. The ploy succeeds. The wedding turns out to be real. Sganarelle has been hoodwinked, but he relents and gives his consent to their union, grateful that his daughter seems to have been miraculously cured. Yet again, love turns out to be the cure for feigned but perhaps genuine lovesickness.

By adopting this approach and effectively wrong-footing those members of the medical profession who came out against love, Molière contributed arguably more than any other to the legitimization of heterosexual culture in France. In the classical age, love was frequently ill-fated, even when it was put on a pedestal by writers like Racine and Madame de Lafayette, but Molière assigns to it a positive value, imparting a new autonomy and naturalness to the notion of the heterosexual couple by freeing them from the shackles of parental authority and medical interference.

The Twentieth Century: The Last Traces of Medical Opposition

Although medical opposition to heterosexual culture decreased progressively with the passage of time, it never disappeared entirely. The medical profession continued to treat with suspicion certain aspects of love and its societal manifestations.

At the close of the nineteenth and the start of the twentieth century, the profession was particularly alarmed by *amour fou*, the "collective insanity" that the poets of the day seemed intent on professing and promoting. It appeared that the surrealist André Breton and others like him had been infected with—and, worse, were wholly oblivious to—the "love madness" that Jacques Ferrand had once described. On the face of it, their excesses and decidedly odd behavior, such as their addiction to automatic writing, appeared to be clear symptoms of an advanced pathological condition. After all, what was one to make of the ramblings of a former medical student who proclaimed that "we Surrealists intend to celebrate the fiftieth anniversary of hysteria, the greatest poetic discovery of the late nineteenth century"?[1] Despite his denials, it was obvious that Breton was seriously ill. Several doctors even volunteered critical diagnoses of his condition (and that of his fellow Surrealists) in much the same way as Ferrand and Jean Aubéry had once taken it on themselves to dissect the works of Pierre de Ronsard and the poets of the Pléiade.

Art, Mysticism, and Erotomania

The term *erotomania*—which many physicians of previous eras (and Ferrand himself in his 1623 treatise *Maladie d'amour*) applied as a synonym for *lovesickness*—was now on everyone's lips. Various medical tracts were devoted to a subject that, for all its superficial modernity, was thus part of a long tradition. *De l'érotomanie*, a doctoral dissertation published in 1902 by A.-E. Portemer, is frequently cited:

> The medical profession has long been intent on studying what philosophers and poets have celebrated as the all-consuming flames of desire: Aristotle with his potions and essences, Solomon's love verging on idolatry, Orpheus venturing deep into Hades in pursuit of his Eurydice, Lucretia stabbing herself through the heart, Tasso and his fourteen-year dream of unrequited love, to say nothing of the relationship between Heloise and Abelard, where erotomania and religion converge and commingle. Erotomania was prevalent in chivalric epics of the Middle Ages and in the Round Table cycle, at a time when women were a veritable cult object and a knight's battle cry was typically "For God and my lady!" . . . And what of Cervantes and his immortal Don Quixote? Is that not an extreme instance of erotomania culminating in eccentricity?[2]

Portemer identified cultural factors as the salient root causes of erotomania, first and foremost among them "the cult object of the female," which, he noted, explained why the Middle Ages and chivalric epics in particular had given rise to such "all-consuming flames of desire." As the principal vectors, or carriers, of that cult, wrote Portemer, poets and writers played a central role in transmitting and spreading the love disorder. (This, one might add, is the same argument that was advanced by Ferrand and Aubéry three centuries previously.)

Art and disorder were now inextricably linked. Often, the artist was erotomanic to the point of hallucination, his or her imagination stimulated by an amalgam of inductive reasoning, free association of ideas, and stream of consciousness. Portemer pointed out that many of those suffering from erotomania were "valued members of society" (writers, poets, artists, teachers) who, to the extent that they possessed fertile imaginations, were uncommonly vulnerable to the condition.

If many artists suffered from erotomania, however, many erotomaniacs were also drawn to art, argued the poet, physician, and psychiatrist Gaston Ferdière in his thesis, "Erotomania." Works of art in general and writing in particular provided a fertile ground for the pathology. Erotomaniacs often exhibited a tendency toward graphorrhea—an obsessive urge to write (letters, poems) that physicians at times encouraged to better understand the origin of the disorder.[3] Portemer, for example, cites the case of Patient B. who obsessively addressed love poems to a certain Miss G. Although Portemer unfortunately does not quote extracts from what, for all one knows, might have been *chefs d'oeuvre*, he notes how frequently what a patient reads is reflected in what he or she writes.[4] Significantly, Ferdière also noted how "strangely similar" letters written by erotomaniacs frequently were,[5] which makes us think that what they had written was replete with clichés and stereotypes drawn from the corpus of romantic literature, where literary masterpieces were perhaps few and far between.

Erotomanic disorder appeared often to take the form of a "dream" or a "sexual urge" directly related to the artist or to the art form itself. Portemer's Miss G., for example, turns out to have been an opera singer, and Gaston Ferdière recalls another patient whose symptoms came to light during a performance of Delibes' *Lakmé* showcasing the talents of the American opera diva Marie Van Zandt.[6] Similarly, French psychiatrists Ernest Dupré and Jean Logre described in their *Les Délires d'imagination* the case of one Miss Corinne, who embarked on a passionate (albeit totally fictive) relationship with "a prominent singer." Elsewhere, in her doctoral thesis investigating two cases of love psychosis,[7] Irène Marcianne Gluck dwelt at length on the case of Odette, who was "romantically involved" with the poet, composer, and singer Léo Ferré.

Although the above and similar case studies demonstrate that erotomania was at the heart of Western love culture and artistic expression, it was also at the heart of religious culture, notably mysticism. Petrus Borellius, court physician to Louis XIV of France, had once written of the close similarity between women who love a man as if he were a god and women who love God as if he were a man. Gaston Ferdière went a step beyond that, driving home the point that, in the final analysis, mysticism was never more than "the illusion of being loved by God." Portemer cites the case of Heloise and Abelard, adding that

> For those familiar with the thought processes of the disordered mind, there can be but little doubt that the ethereal devotion that priests exhibit toward the Virgin Mary and that is observed frequently in many serious theological treatises can be sourced to an unwitting and unconscious erotomania. It is a love for women that is ardently expressed by these virtuous bachelors under the guise of piety. Their aberrant behavior is easily explained by their chastity. Who among us can ever forget Émile Zola's masterly description of Abbé Mouret's "transgression" as he stands before the Virgin, his lips quivering in anticipation as she approaches him?

As evidence, Portemer then appends an *in extenso* two-page extract from Zola's *La Faute de l'abbé Mouret*, documenting the priest's adoration of a Virgin "bathed in sunlight" with "the milk of infinite love falling drop by drop from her maidenly breast."

This view of mysticism as a form of erotomania is consistent in that, as pointed out earlier, devotion to the Virgin was often expressed in a form borrowed from the cult of heterosexual love. The suggestion that the cult of the Virgin may itself be a kind of erotomania, whether justified or otherwise, indicates how far the medical profession at the turn of the twentieth century had moved beyond Aubéry and Ferrand, neither of whom could have entertained such a suggestion. The perceived iconoclasm reflects the march of science, whose most committed opponent—particularly at the time of the Third Republic—had been religion. Deep down, the medical profession continued to be suspicious of heterosexuality, but now it was even more suspicious of religion.

Erotomania: From the Liver to the Brain

There is a wealth of further evidence to document the extent to which the medical profession of the nineteenth and early twentieth century had changed and broken with tradition. Like their counterparts in the sixteenth and seventeenth centuries, members of the profession recognized that gender, age, and heredity were factors to be taken into account in diagnosing and treating illnesses and physical disorders. Unlike their predecessors, however, they refused to endorse the once immutable conviction that love was somehow a function of "body heat."

At the same time, they challenged the received wisdom that the locus of love disorders was the liver or the uterus. The nineteenth-century doctor and psychiatrist Jean-Étienne Dominique Esquirol refuted this theory in the strongest possible terms, arguing that erotomania was a condition of the mind and that, logically, its locus must be in the head. Portemer shared this view but proved incapable of taking it much further: "I have said it lies in the head, but where? In the brain? I profess ignorance and admit I do not know."[8]

The physicians of the twentieth century were as much in the dark as their predecessors in the Renaissance when it came to defining erotomania, its source, and the ways that it affected the body as a whole. It was "in the brain," and that was all there was to it. Yet the term *erotomania* found a place in the medical vocabulary and was progressively substituted for the traditional term *lovesickness*, which seemed archaic and arcane and carried literary and populist connotations. Given its Greek origins, the term *erotomania* somehow sounded more medical (and the *-mania* tag clearly indicated that one was dealing with a kind of madness or aberration). The emphasis had shifted from the physiological to the psychiatric: the liver was out, and the brain was in. Doctors and psychiatrists continued to point to the decisive role in society of art and culture, but art, religion, and love remained eminently suspect in their eyes.

Late nineteenth-century medical psychiatrists proved particularly adept at exploring hitherto virgin psychic territory, describing new kinds of mental disorders, and coining new terminology (of which *heterosexuality* was a striking example). In *The Invention of Heterosexuality*, American historian Jonathan Ned Katz reveals that, as late as 1923, the term *heterosexuality* referred to a "morbid sexual passion for one of the opposite sex."[9] He also cites one preeminent St. Louis physician, speaking in 1893, who felt confident enough to reassure colleagues that, by medical treatment, reason and emotions could be "turned back into normal channels, the homo and hetero sexual changed into beings of natural erotic inclination, with normal impulses."[10]

Even a cursory examination of dictionaries published around this time is highly revealing. As late as 1901, for instance, *Dorland's Medical Dictionary* defined *heterosexuality* as "Abnormal or perverted appetite toward the opposite sex."[11] The 1923 definition quoted on the previous page is from Merriam-Webster's *New International Dictionary*. Clearly, heterosexuality was a disorder that deserved to be taken seriously. At the time, sexual typology was straightforward: there were homosexuals, who felt a morbid attraction to persons of their own sex; heterosexuals, who experienced a morbid attraction to members of the opposite sex; and normal people, who thought of sex as neither special nor autonomous but simply married (as and when possible), went on to have children together, and did their best to remain on good terms with their respective partners.

Today, the term *heterosexual* no longer describes a pathologically deviant condition but is applied instead to the social norm. It is instructive to explore how this evolution came about (something that Jonathan Ned Katz fails to do in his otherwise remarkable study).

As the present pages suggest, this semantic about-face can be explained only from the perspective of history. At the end of the nineteenth century, the medical profession continued to adhere to medieval traditions by condemning sexual passion, the celebration of which they, like their predecessors, held to be contrary to sound mental health. Then, as noted above, there was a major shift in emphasis away from the physiological to the psychiatric model as the locus of disorder was displaced from the liver to the brain. For all that, the medical fraternity continued to view the celebration of heterosexuality and the heterosexual couple as "unwholesome" and "morbid." It was then that psychiatry reprised the term *erotomania* (which had for a long time been used to describe lovesickness) and postulated a new synonym—heterosexuality.

In effect, the medical fraternity was already fighting a rear-guard action. Heterosexuality, traditionally condemned by physicians as a pathological tendency, had long since become the dominant cultural norm and had been embraced as such by the lay public. Accordingly, medical practitioners hastened to discard the previous (and now outmoded and discredited) heterosexual/homosexual/normal typology in favor of a two-term sociocultural paradigm that, predictably, declared heterosexuals to be normal people (as opposed to homosexuals, who were not).

In his benchmark *Das Problem der Homosexualität und sexueller Perversionen* of 1917, Alfred Adler argued that homosexuality "negates the human will to perpetuate the species," adding that "this simple fact is enough to justify the imposition of heterosexual behavior as the norm and consider aberrant, sinful or criminal every perversion, including that of masturbation." Far from viewing heterosexuality and homosexuality as "symmetrical" disorders, Adler was adamant that heterosexuality now be accepted as the norm and homosexuality declared perverted or "sinful"— the latter designation hinting at a convergence of medical and religious opinion. To the extent that Adler's opinion was widely accepted and endorsed, the term *heterosexuality* was then progressively used in the sense familiar to us today. What was once a disorder became the norm.

Love as an Opiate for Women

Although the medical profession as a whole may have continued to voice reservations until comparatively recently, it is clear that the first stirrings of the feminist movement in France helped enlist its support for the heterosexual cause.

As of the close of the nineteenth century, women were increasingly represented in professions, such as the medical profession, that were formerly regarded as male strongholds. The first women interns were admitted in 1887, and others soon followed, upsetting once and for all the traditional structure of the profession and sending shock waves through its hitherto exclusively male ranks and through society generally. Many novels written around this time featured "lady doctors," in most instances mocking their aspirations to do something that they were biologically unsuited for and that interfered with their duty to love and be loved.

The historian Juliette Rennes has noted in this regard that "several novels featuring women doctors exhibited a major concern that their newfound familiarity with the human anatomy would somehow dissipate the mystique and magic attaching to the act of love."[12] Plot lines were virtually standard, noted Rennes: a highly intelligent woman studies medicine, graduates as a doctor, and sacrifices conjugal bliss on the altar of a professional career.

Thus, in *Princesses de science*, first published in 1907 and translated into English two years later as *The Doctor Wife*, Catholic novelist Colette Yver's heroine Thérèse Guéméné, the daughter of a celebrated surgeon, is so preoccupied with her own burgeoning career as a doctor that, to her husband Fernand's dismay, she neglects her domestic duties and professes to be too busy to breast-feed their baby who, deprived of mother's milk, ultimately dies. In the end, Thérèse comes to her senses, gives up any pretension to fame and fortune as a doctor, and reverts to her proper role as "a wife whose career is of no consequence by comparison with the love she bears for her husband." Colette Yver wrote several novels in this vein, implicitly critical of those she dismissed as *cervellines*—women whose "brains had atrophied their hearts" and who were feminine in name only, incapable of love.[13]

The argument that women were genetically and emotionally predisposed to love was a cross between late eighteenth-century Rousseauism and late nineteenth-century science. Women were asked to stay at home because of their biological nature as well as their disposition for love. The two elements were often inseparable: love was part of woman's nature, and woman's nature was defined by science.

On the face of it, this attitude was more palatable than the condescension and tyranny implicit in arguments habitually adduced in justification of male dominance. That women could find happiness in domesticity and the *status quo* was anything but a new idea, however, nor was it greeted with any particular show of enthusiasm: over and above domesticity, women were now being promised love, albeit with their own husbands.

From Tristan and Iseult to the Surrealists, writers had never shown any great interest in conjugal love. Admittedly, marrying for love had been socially acceptable ever since Erasmus, but in cultural terms, it had never made its mark with poets and artists. (Only in rare instances in Romantic literature, for example, are the ideal lover and the ideal husband one and the same.) Now, a new generation of authors seemed intent on convincing women of the glories of conjugal love, while at the same time, the medical fraternity was at pains to provide a scientific basis for it, not least because doing so might help protect its own profession from a potential influx of competitive career-minded women.

The argument that women should spontaneously and naturally accept the subservient social status allotted them had self-evident flaws and limitations, not least since it had typically been applied much less consistently elsewhere in comparable circumstances of social imbalance. There had sometimes been discursive attempts to reconcile black and white, rich and poor, Christian and Muslim and to generate a climate of empathy and cooperation that would conceal and facilitate power relations. In the nineteenth century, for example, the paternalist attitude of some employers was intended to sublimate or repress the socioeconomic relationship between themselves and their workforce. Similarly, since the sixteenth century, missionaries had frequently tried to rationalize colonial conquest in terms of Christian charity, the conviction that one was somehow responsible for the spiritual welfare of one's fellow man (although slavery and the wholesale massacre of indigenous peoples tended to suggest otherwise).

The palliative argument that was now being advanced in respect of women and love must be regarded as a deliberate bid to encourage female acquiescence while dissimulating (and, in consequence, reinforcing) male dominance. As such, it has turned out to be not wholly ineffectual, since it continued to prove an inconvenience to (heterosexual) feminists well into the 1970s and even beyond, persuading at least some that a choice had to be made between love and equality and many others to argue that the very notion of equality is inimical to heterosexual love. These fears were compounded given that some men were quick to seize any opportunity to escalate the war of the sexes. But in reality, love was their best enemy: love was an opiate for women.

The Pathology of Homosexuality

The belief that heterosexual love was the most natural thing in the world was accorded widespread acceptance and approval as the twentieth century progressed. Even so, the nascent discipline of psychoanalysis soon called the notion into question.

In his *Three Essays on the Theory of Sexuality* published in 1905, Sigmund Freud argued the probability that heterosexuality was not a given:

Thus from the point of view of psycho-analysis the exclusive sexual interest felt by men for women is also a problem that needs elucidating and is not a self-evident fact based upon an attraction that is ultimately of a chemical nature.[14]

Far from being natural in biological or biochemical terms, therefore, heterosexuality and homosexuality were, in Freud's submission, functions of an individual's personal psychic makeup.

In his discussion of "polymorphously perverse" infantile bisexuality, Freud argued that heterosexuality was the result of a long and arduous psychic apprenticeship extending far back into earliest childhood. This assertion subsequently appeared elsewhere in his work, where he argued that "normal sexuality too depends upon a restriction in the choice of object."[15] In other words, although never going to the lengths that psychiatry once had and dismissing heterosexuality as a pathological condition, psychoanalysis was at pains to show that it was not an inborn characteristic. Analysis of every single complex—not least the Oedipus variety—tended to confirm this. Despite broad dissemination and awareness of psychoanalytical theory, however, the vast majority of the public (and most psychoanalysts) remained unaware of the notion that heterosexuality or, indeed, homosexuality was an acquired condition.

Since medical science was persuaded that heterosexuality was natural, very few took practitioners the trouble to inquire whether attraction to the opposite sex came about as the result of an organ, a hormone, a gene, or some other physiological mechanism. Instead, medical research tended to be directed toward the causes of attraction between members of the same sex—toward different, abnormal, and inexplicable behavior (that is, homosexual, an antithetical term coined only a few years before *heterosexual*).

In previous centuries, sodomy had not unduly preoccupied the medical profession but from the middle of the nineteenth century, a massive investigation was launched into homosexuality in all its forms and manifestations. Early research into the causes of homosexuality were conducted by alienists, mental pathologists, and psychiatrists such as Richard von Krafft-Ebbing, who, as Pierre-Olivier de Busscher has pointed out, played a central role in probing the clinical causes of homosexuality: "The central figure in psychiatry's appropriation of homosexuality was Richard von Krafft-Ebing, the Austrio-German psychiatrist. His famous work *Psychopathia Sexualis*, a study of sexual perversity, was first published in 1886, then constantly updated throughout the next century, even after his death by his disciple Albert Moll."[16]

From Krafft-Ebbing's *Psychopathia sexualis*, homosexuality emerges as the classic example of "sexual perversion" and constitutes a pattern for all other perversions: it is a congenital, morbid hereditary disorder, the product of *dégénérescence* (degenerating lineage or bloodline) and gender inversion. Some took this even further, among them Valentin Magnan, for example, who held that homosexuality was a cerebrospinal disorder caused by reduced sensory perception due to a malfunctioning of the posterior cortex. The alleged existence of a so-called homosexual brain was used to justify all manner of subsequent twentieth century medical procedures, including lobotomy, electroshock, and various other treatments (such as aversion therapy and the like).

Some looked to the brain as the root cause and locus of homosexuality, whereas others suspected some form of glandular or hormonal imbalance. Endocrinology came into its own around the turn of the century as researchers struggled to identify and isolate sexual hormones, such as estrogens, progesterone, and testosterone. In 1929, Ernst Laqueur discovered female hormones in samples of male urine, triggering speculation that homosexuality resulted from hormonal imbalance and that, by extension, it was a condition that might be alleviated or cured by adjusting male and female hormone counts. It came as something of a disappointment that this form of treatment proved less than satisfactory: as it happened, it yielded disastrous results when tested on human guinea pigs. Over time, however, occasional forms of therapy proved popular with certain members of the medical profession, including Danish endocrinologist Carl Værnet, who, as an SS major, conducted glandular experiments in Buchenwald concentration camp under the direct authority of Reichsführer Heinrich Himmler.

Endocrinology and psychiatry may have played their part, but a number of advances in terms of diagnosing the causes of homosexuality came in the field of genetics. Since the days of Richard von Krafft-Ebing and the Austrian-born French psychiatrist Bénédict Augustin Morel, issues of hereditary morbidity and degenerescence had been widely discussed in medical and scientific literature. Thus, in 1904, Ernst Rüdin (the German-Swiss psychiatrist who in 1933 served as a member of Himmler's notorious Task Force on Heredity) recommended that homosexuals be sterilized to protect the Aryan race. Various genetic studies were then conducted to establish whether homosexuality could be diagnosed prior to birth, at which possibility the specter of eugenics raised its head.[17] None of these investigations yielded a positive outcome, a fact that persuaded Dr. Paul Cameron, leader of the U.S.-based Conservative Political Action Conference, to declare in 1985, "Unless we get medically lucky, in three or four years, one of the options discussed will be the extermination of homosexuals."[18]

On May 17, 1990, after decades of biomedical research into causes and potential cures for homosexuality, the World Health Organization finally conceded that homosexuality was not a disorder or disease.[19] It emerged that research in this field had proved not only "scientifically"[20] inconclusive but had frequently been "therapeutically catastrophic." Despite this, so-called restorative therapies persisted in numerous parts of the world.[21] What is remarkable is that theories were tested specifically with regard to homosexuality in particular rather than sexual orientation in general. In other words, the key area of heterosexuality was left essentially unexplored. The objective had once again been to account for the different and the abnormal. And once again, that objective had proved unattainable.[22]

Psychoanalysis—which lies at the fringes of medicine *sensu stricto*— has also offered a number of possible explanations for homosexuality. These (hypo)theses are all too familiar—sexual regression, infantile fixation, Oedipal identification with a parent of the same sex, inversion/ perversion, and so on. Taken together, these pseudoacademic theories represent a litany of explanations rehashed and routinely trotted out in twentieth-century educational sex manuals for use by mothers who fear their child may be in danger of growing up homosexual. Once again, as is often the case, the focus of speculation is not only on what causes homosexuality but also on what means exist to counter it.

Teaching Heterosexuality

The various hypotheses articulated by psychoanalysts had a considerable practical impact on society as a whole and, more particularly, on the field of education. Although there may have been little interest in what actually caused heterosexuality, there was a deep-rooted determination to safeguard and promote it, especially among the young. It was argued that, if normal sexuality (that is, heterosexuality) was the result of an evolutionary process or what Freud had referred to as an "apprenticeship," then it surely followed that heterosexuality could—and should perhaps—be taught in some form or other.

It was considered too important a subject to be left to chance, however. Accordingly, the twentieth century as a whole saw what purported to be "progressive scientific research" led by pedagogues anxious on the one hand to engender and promote heterosexuality at childhood level (declaring it to be absolutely natural) and, on the other, to suppress potential causes of homosexuality (a condition they regarded as clearly against nature). Naturalness had to be constructed through social engineering at the price of this double paradox.

Conservative theorists were not alone in advocating education along these lines. In *Der sexuelle Kampf der Jugend* (The Sexual Struggle of Youth), a pamphlet published in 1932, Austrian-born sexologist Wilhelm Reich—whose work was to exert great influence on the younger generation in the 1960s generally and on the May 1968 French protests in particular—attempted to explain how adolescent heterosexuality might be encouraged. Elsewhere, educator and founder of Summerhill School A. S. Neill published his benchmark *Summerhill: A Radical Approach to Child Rearing* in 1960 and promptly triggered a wave of pedagogical experimentation throughout Europe and beyond. Neill was convinced his "progressive" approach had brought results, asserting that "over a period of forty years, the school has not turned out a single homosexual. The reason is that freedom breeds healthy children."[23]

Meanwhile, "progressives" who advocated the incorporation of sex education into school curricula were, by and large, concerned that instruction be given in heterosexuality, which is to say, exclusively in the rudiments of heterosexual reproduction and contraception. The basics of heterosexual culture had to be taught in the classroom. This was more often than not a task for biology teachers (as recommended, for example, in France's Fontanet Circular of 1973). The wheel had turned full circle: science, which had once opposed the spread of heterosexual culture, now supported its propagation via the educational system.

Advances in medical science helped generate an image of the typical homosexual (something that Foucault and others pointed out) and of the typical heterosexual. To the extent that heterosexuality had come to be unreservedly viewed as natural, social norms had now undergone radical change. At one point in history, men had been recommended to eschew female company for fear of becoming (or being regarded as) effeminate (a gender issue) or, in the eyes of the Roman Catholic Church, guilty of debauchery (a sex issue). Now, however, men were encouraged to seek out the company of women for fear of being regarded as homosexual. The issue was now one of both gender and sex: the latter because the homosexual was *ipso facto* debauched, and the former because he was of necessity effeminate.

Certain practical educational reforms were undertaken to reflect medical and psychoanalytical theory. Ever since publication of Tissot's celebrated *L'Onanisme* (*Onanism*), pedagogues had favored boarding schools as a means of providing an alternative education to that provided by parents who, among other things, were allegedly incapable of discouraging masturbatory tendencies in their offspring. Taking action against the "sin of Onan" carried with it another and perhaps even greater risk, however—that of "special friendships." Since boarding schools were single-sex institutions, it was found that mutual masturbatory behavior (initially among boys but latterly also among girls, once it was eventually thought desirable to educate the female sex) tended to trigger same-sex adolescent emotions such as that celebrated in Roger Peyrefitte's 1943 novel *Special Friendships* or in Henry de Montherlant's 1952 play *The Fire That Consumes*. Montherlant was himself sent down from college in Sainte-Croix de Neuilly for precisely this reason. Catholic colleges had reputations to protect, as had military schools, where, according to Pierre Albertini, "any student 'found in a bed other than one's own' was [until recently] subject to punishment, usually grounding."[24]

The concepts of physician Simon-Auguste Tissot (*Onanism: Or a Treatise on the Disorders Produced by Masturbation*, 1760), and later Ambroise Tardieu (*Étude médico-légale sur les attentats aux mœurs* [Medical-Legal Studies of Assaults against Decency], 1857) long influenced school authorities in France. According to Tissot, any sexual act that does not lead to procreation causes physical weakness, while Tardieu believed that the true pederasts, who were few in numbers, corrupted the rest, who became "occasional" homosexuals. Acting on this, the heads of boarding schools (both public and private) increased the supervision of dormitories (in a way that never took place in England, where it was believed that character was built through self-policing) with the clear intention of preventing all sexual activity. Monseigneur Dupanloup once said that a dormitory supervisor had two obsessions, "special friendships and improper familiarities," and that he had to maintain at all times the rule of *numquam duo* (never in twos). In 1876, criminologist Cesare Lombroso echoed a similar affirmation in his *L'Uomo delinquente* (*Criminal Man*): "When you see two young men together, be wary, they are probably up to no good." Author George Sand reminds us that this rule applied also to girls, around the beginning of the nineteenth century: "We were forbidden to go off together in twos, it had to be three. We were not allowed to embrace. They worried about our innocent communications."[25]

It would appear that strict supervision and close monitoring were not enough to guarantee the (heterosexual) development of French youth. Two of France's leading university-level establishments of higher education (one *école normale* in the Rue d'Ulm in Paris for young men and the other in Sèvres for young girls) were supposed to set an example to other educational establishments but were in fact widely reputed to be breeding grounds for homosexuals.

Coeducation was proposed as a possible solution. As Pierre Albertini rightly pointed out, there is a tendency to forget that the notion of mixed schools was first mooted in 1872 by French chemist Henri Sainte-Claire Deville, the aim being to root out what current medical terminology referred to as the "terrible perversion of instincts" that were in his view inevitable when adolescents of the same sex were under one roof.[26] Thus, when the concept of coeducation was aired at the end of the nineteenth century, it was not to promote sexual equality, which was not on the social agenda at the time, but to encourage the heterosexual development of children and adolescents of both sexes.[27] Wilhelm Reich also recommended that girls and boys be educated together to expand their respective heterosexual horizons and, by implication, curb any homosexual tendencies.

However, at the same time as coeducation was being heralded as a solution to "special friendships" (a sex issue), it was also recognized as potentially harmful to the differences between the sexes (a gender issue). Various authorities on the subject suggested that mixed instruction might even efface the distinctive traits of either sex, effectively making boys appear more effeminate and girls more masculine (a gender issue). The resultant gender identity confusion might then cause a sexual problem in the form of "mutual disaffection" (a sex issue).[28] To prevent this, a number of single-sex activities were introduced. In periods devoted to physical education, for example, boys were encouraged to climb ropes to develop muscle and upper-body strength, whereas girls were taught eurhythmics to promote grace and elegance. By the same token, technical instruction might take the form of carpentry or metalworking for boys and domestic science or needlework for girls. The objective behind this deliberate diversification was to ensure that sexual coeducation did not give rise to gender-identity issues.

Heterosexuality: A Scientific Obsession

Medicine and school played a major role in the process of "heterosexualization" of youth. On the whole, however, and although most people accepted heterosexuality as natural and normal, it was felt strongly that nature should be allowed to take its course. In other words, doctors and teachers were at pains to identify how a taste for the opposite sex might most safely and effectively be cultivated while at the same time warding off potential threats such as masturbation, homosexuality, and gender-identity disorders.

All three threats could arguably be sourced to the issue of homosexuality as understood in the broadest possible sense. After all, what was masturbation if not an extreme form of homosexual behavior where the sex object was oneself? And what was gender-identity disorder if not an equally extreme form of homosexuality? If boys and girls engaged in exactly the same activities in school to the point where the former became effeminate and the latter virile, wouldn't the net result be an indifference between the sexes leading to a generalized homosexuality? Everything pointed in one direction: homosexuality had to be rooted out. And no effort to do so would be spared.

Medicine, which in the Middle Ages and under the Ancien Régime had been of comparatively less interest and had taken a back seat to heroic ethos and religious debate, was now firmly in the driving seat in matters of sex and gender. "Scientific" medicine had come of age and, in a certain sense, had taken over where chivalry and Church had left off, the principal difference in the twentieth century being that the medical profession—far from opposing heterosexual culture as warriors and churchmen had traditionally done—was among its staunchest advocates.

The language of psychiatry and psychoanalysis was replete with technical terms, but the message was sufficiently accessible when transmitted via such diverse channels and networks as the formal educational system, shared-interest associations, sporting bodies, summer camps, parental sex instruction manuals, women's magazines, general-interest psychology publications, popular science and technology journals, adolescent literature, and many more vehicles besides, all of them viable conduits for the dissemination of heterosexual culture. In the final analysis there was consensus that, as novelist Marguerite Duras once wrote, "passion can *only* be heterosexual."

Medicine played a defining role in postulating behavioral norms calculated to promote moral, physical, and sexual health among children and youth. In this instance, the terminology may have been distinctly less technical, but the underlying aim of protecting the young was couched in a sort of scientific vulgate that, for all its rational, secular, and republican overtones, was never all that different from the Christian moralizing it was intended to replace.

The problems inherent in promoting heterosexuality and eradicating homosexuality were nowhere more evident than in the humanities, where teachers were frequently required to expose pupils and students to material that did not conform to the accepted standards of the day. One initial response lay in obfuscation or simply ignoring the most insidious material. But it was never a serious option to jettison the whole corpus of classical literature. In this respect, another technique was indicated—mutilation. In most instances, this took the form of expurgating *ad usum delphini*, removing material that was considered potentially offensive or harmful to the young. Accordingly, the works of Sappho, Anacreon, Pindar, Catullus, Virgil, Horace, Tibullus, Martial, and so on were sanitized and revamped to conform to heterosexual expectations.

A third technique was out-and-out falsification, typically by the simple expedient of altering names and changing the gender of personal pronouns. This was the case with Michelangelo, whose verse came to light only to be hidden away by his descendants for the better part of sixty years. When the texts were finally published, the sonnets addressed to his lover Tommaso dei Cavalieri were abbreviated and purged to suggest that the object of his affection was a woman. One example should suffice to illustrate the deception: the line "I am held captive by an armed knight" is neatly amended to "I am held captive by a virtuous heart." It was not until 1897 that a German scholar named Karl Frey examined the manuscript and restored the text to its original form. It had been hidden away, then truncated and finally falsified—could there have been a more obvious example of *post mortem* sexual therapy?

Authors were frequently heterosexualized by being put, so to speak, under the knife of philology. In other instances, however, it was sometimes enough merely to shift the interpretative emphasis so as to influence a prospective (young) reader's response. Shakespeare's *Sonnets*, published in 1609, are particularly revealing in this respect. The initial 126 love poems are addressed to a young man, the following twenty-four to a mysterious "Dark Lady." In 1640, John Benson reissued the sonnets as a collection of *Poems*, where *he* and *his* were substituted by *she* and *her*. To the extent that the reading public was already familiar with the original version, Benson's inept reworking actually drew attention to the homoerotic element he was anxious to conceal. Some contemporary critics offered the rather lame explanation that the original 1609 quarto version was ambiguous and "merely reflected Elizabethan usage." Samuel Taylor Coleridge, for one, was confused: he initially endorsed the interpretation that held that the sonnets were addressed to a young man but subsequently backtracked, insisting that the male pronouns were no more than a deliberate device to mislead the reader. François-Victor Hugo (Victor's son), who later translated the poems into French, speculated that those that were addressed to the young man might in fact have been written by a tearful female admirer who was not identified elsewhere in the collection.

The *Sonnets* caused problems not because they were a celebration of homosexual love but because the individual who wrote them (homosexual or bisexual as the case may be) was called William Shakespeare. Written by anyone else, the poems would in all probability have been consigned to the dustbin of history, but accepting that they were authored by the iconic Shakespeare was impossible for many, since this was tantamount to conceding that the bard was possibly a pervert and a sodomite. Could pupils and students conceivably be exposed to that unpalatable truth? The answer was a resounding no. Remedial therapy was called for, analogous to that meted out to hospitalized nineteenth- and twentieth-century homosexuals.

Shakespeare was by no means an isolated case. Historically, obfuscation, adulteration, falsification, and misdirection were often used in posthumous attempts to heterosexualize a given author. It would be an error to conclude that these techniques were no longer common at the end of the twentieth century. In 1998, for example, I was retained by a well-known publisher to contribute to a literary compendium. I duly proposed inclusion in the collection of a few pages on *Les Fleurs du mal* together with two or three paragraphs on Baudelaire's treatment of women. I was presumptuous enough to point out that Baudelaire had at one point considered *Les Lesbiennes* as one of several possible alternative titles and that he had written some Sapphic verse that was formally banned in 1857. The editor informed me in no uncertain terms that it would be entirely inappropriate to introduce this subject, particularly in a work addressed to younger readers. He also pointed out that there was already a plethora of school texts on Baudelaire's women (true) that did not raise the subject of lesbianism (not untrue). I carried on regardless.

Heterosexuality: A Political Obsession

The interface between heterosexual culture and politics is exemplified by conservative politician Baroness Young, the first-ever female leader of the U.K. House of Lords, known in later life for her vociferous and sustained crusade against gay rights. Specifically, Baroness Young campaigned long and hard (although ultimately in vain) against the repeal of section 28 of the Local Government Act of 1988, which held that a local authority should not intentionally promote homosexuality, publish or make available to schools and public libraries any material that did so, or promote the teaching in any "maintained" (i.e., state-funded) school of the "acceptability of homosexuality as a pretended family relationship."

Elsewhere, in 1995, a school in the U.S. state of New Hampshire issued a ruling prohibiting teachers from discussing gay and lesbian issues in a positive way. This move was directly inspired by a homophobic amendment tabled some years previously by Senator Jesse Helms and designed to preclude federal funding of any materials liable to "promote or encourage, directly or indirectly, homosexual sexual activities." (The amendment was defeated in Congress.) As for erstwhile French Prime Minister Edith Cresson, she came down energetically on the side of heterosexuality, loudly proclaiming that "heterosexuality is better!"

The overriding ambition was to impose heterosexual values on society generally and young people in particular by making the educational system as a whole into a vehicle for the dissemination and naturalization of heterosexual culture. Canonical authors who needed it were offered a symbolic therapy—a kind of heterosexual makeup. This was never more evident than during the debate on how homosexuality might best be addressed in schools. Although there was broad support among intellectuals and militants for the incorporation of gay and lesbian issues into academic curricula and despite positive guidelines on sex education, homophobia, and the battle against AIDS announced by successive French education ministers such as Jack Lang and Luc Ferry, no genuinely substantive changes were ever introduced.

The demands of the gay and lesbian communities remained in any event unpalatable to conservatives, who continued to assert the dominance of heterosexuality over homosexuality. As liberal democrat Jean-François

Mattéi claimed, "there can be no equivalence between heterosexual and homosexual couples. This statement is obvious and has nothing to do with any kind of moral or fundamentalist considerations." Professor Mattéi was absolutely right, if only to the extent that he was content to rely on nineteenth-century medical ideology, but that did not render his opinion any less homophobic.

Many progressive thinkers also considered it inconceivable that a place—however modest—might be found within the educational establishment for gay and lesbian issues. According to them, at best schools should remain strictly neutral in sexual matters and abstain from endorsing any particular sexual orientation whatsoever. Their attitude was thus resolutely secular and republican. The myth of educational neutrality and objectivity in sexual matters might be considered laughable by some, however, bearing in mind the lengthy process of heterosexualization described in these pages and elsewhere. That said, the diversity of opinions sincerely held and expressed attests to the undoubted impact of heterosexual culture and, moreover, its tacit acceptance as a standard component of the educational system. There was nothing particularly odd about this, since people had become conditioned to accept heterosexuality a priori as the natural expression of human sexuality as a whole and found it impossible to think of it as anything other than a way of life. That heterosexuality might be both a beacon and a blindspot does not seem to have occurred to them.

In ultraconservative circles, the spread of heterosexual culture has often seemed less relevant than the unchecked proliferation of invasive gay and lesbian values. Thus, in 1998, Avenir de la Culture—a French association set up to promote and protect "family values"—complained that "homosexuality and all the sexual perversions that have infiltrated literature, film, theater, and the media generally, represent an attack against which young people in particular have no adequate defense."

This allegation must be rebutted on at least three fronts. First, this resolutely right-wing Christian association resorted—significantly—to outmoded psychiatric terminology, such as "sexual perversions," a formulation dating back to the days of Krafft-Ebing and his *Psychopathia sexualis*. Second, the association implicitly paralleled homosexuality and pedophilia in a bid to mobilize and maximize public support (and, in so doing, revealed how crucial the issue of youth was to those determined to champion the cause of public heterosexuality). And, third, it showed how closely aligned the association was with anti-PACS campaigners[29] who deplored the extent to which homosexuality had invaded books, film, theater, and so on.

The association's name—The Future of Culture—could just as well have been amended to read The Future of Heterosexual Culture.

Medical Opinion and the Future of Heterosexual Culture

By the start of the twentieth century, heterosexuality and the entrenched opinions of the medical profession with regard to it had been called into question. The new brand of criticism differed radically from what had gone before. Previously, criticism had rested on the acknowledged authority of religious ethics, chivalric codes, and to a lesser extent medical discourse. Now, criticisms of heterosexuality appeared to be based on marginal or dissident opinions used to deconstruct received medical opinion regarding sexuality. In other words, former criticisms rested on the dominant order against the emergent culture of heterosexuality, while now they constituted an emergent discourse facing the dominant heterosexual order. Conservative (in the nonpejorative sense) gave way to progressive (in the nonameliorative sense) as medical opposition to heterosexual culture was substituted by homosexual opposition to medical culture.

In France, André Gide was doubtless among the first to question the tacit acceptance of heterosexual culture. In 1924, he published *Corydon*, a sequence of four Socratic dialogs he later described as the most important of his books. His aim was to examine preconceived notions of sexuality and biology and to challenge prevalent biomedical orthodoxy:

> Just think how in our society, in our behavior, everything predestines one sex to the other; everything teaches heterosexuality, everything urges it upon us, everything provokes us to it: theater, literature, newspapers, the paraded example set by our elders, the ritual of our drawing rooms and our street corners. "Given all that, failing to fall in love is a sign of ill breeding!," crows Dumas *fils* in his preface to *La*

Question d'argent. Yet if a young man finally succumbs to so much collusion in the world around him, you refuse to grant that his decision was influenced, his desire manipulated if he ends up making his choice in the "right" direction! And if, in spite of advice, invitations, provocations of all kinds, he should manifest a homosexual tendency, you immediately blame his reading or some other influence (and you argue in the same way for an entire nation, an entire people); it has to be an acquired taste, you insist; he must have been taught it.[30]

Gide did not believe in allegedly innate heterosexual attraction. For him, the psychological roots of heterosexuality were inseparable from the social norms and conventions that formed it. That being so, heterosexuality was not simply a given. In this respect, Gide's views were to some extent close to certain of Freud's conclusions as to the problematic nature of heterosexuality. Not that it mattered at the time, however, given that society and its institutions were based on tacitly accepted and "self-evident" truths and that the vast majority of people continued to use the language of heterosexuality without ever pausing to reflect on its origins or its consequences.

Since the 1970s, however, the expanding feminist movement returned to the question from a fresh perspective, arguing that an entrenched system of heterosexual culture was closely bound up with the notion of male dominance, which they were determined to oppose. In her *Sexual Politics* of 1970, radical feminist Kate Millett attacked what she termed "the heterosexual caste system,"[31] which had spawned a social hierarchy based on sexuality. Homosexual movements are frequently accused of proselytizing, but Millett took another tack by denouncing "a rabid sort of heterosexual activis[ts]"[32] who were determined to confer sexual legitimacy on a specific group.

Gayle Rubin adopted a similar approach in her 1975 essay "The Traffic in Women: Notes on the 'Political Economy' of Sex," excoriating the "compulsory heterosexuality" imposed on individuals from a very early age. As she was also refusing the illusion of "nature," she insisted on the contrary on the social and sexual process that creates the conditions of its own denial.[33]

Mention should also be made of other important contributors to the debate, notably Adrienne Rich, whose "Compulsory Heterosexuality and Lesbian Existence" was published in 1980, and Monique Wittig, author of *The Straight Mind.* The "straight mind" is understood as a political system based on the subjection of women and the heterosexual injunction. As a result, Wittig's critique is less about patriarchy than heterosexuality. Women, she argues, must "break off the heterosexual contract."[34]

The gender studies and queer studies that emerged in the United States throughout the 1980s and 1990s also marginally touched on the issue of heterosexuality. In "Imitation and Gender Insubordination" (1991), philosopher Judith Butler deconstructs the notion of sexual identity (*a fortiori* heterosexuality), arguing that "heterosexuality is an impossible imitation of itself, an imitation that performatively constitutes itself as the original."[35] As a matter of fact, any sexual identity, whether heterosexual or homosexual, is no more than the more or less conscious imitation of existing stereotypes, which are themselves constituted on the basis of other stereotypes imitating other imitations, according to an infinite movement toward an illusory origin. Although trying to pass as natural, heterosexuality is a "gender performance," a staging of oneself, modeling the subject on the pattern of an unlikely original.

Heterosexism, a concept on which I elaborated at length in my *Dictionary of Homophobia,* comes at considerable social cost—not only because it excludes homosexuals but also because it includes heterosexuals whether they like it or not. Young seventeen-year-old heterosexual males who have as yet no girlfriend, unmarried women in their mid-twenties, divorcees, and widows: they all suffer on account of the perceived difference between themselves and the heterosexual norm. There are also those who actually live in heterosexual relationships but who sacrifice their innermost desires and free will on the altar of collective "normality."

One might go even further and ask—as do certain Christian groups such as Avenir de la Culture—whether heterosexual culture is under threat in and of itself and as a hegemonic system. This question is entirely separate from the fact that homosexuals and homosexual culture may enjoy a higher profile than before: in effect, the threat (if it indeed exists) is more fundamental. Traditionally, heterosexual culture has found its principal justification in the link between sexuality and reproduction.

Since it takes two people, one from each sex, to procreate, heterosexual practices have been validated as indispensable for purposes of reproduction and sustaining birthrates.[36]

The obvious link between sexuality and reproduction has been seriously attenuated in contemporary Western society. On the one hand, there are new techniques and technologies (intrauterine devices, contraceptives, the morning-after pill, and the widespread legalization of abortion) that foster nonreproductive sex practices, while, on the other, there are different processes (such as in vitro fertilization, test-tube babies, and—why not?—the future possibility of *ex utero* birth and even cloning) that favor nonsexual reproduction. As a result, sexuality and reproduction promise to move even further apart than they are at present.

What might this scenario imply in the longer term? The triumph of heterosexual autonomy? The eclipse of heterosexual culture's historical legitimacy? In other words, could heterosexual culture be on the way out? Certainly not, but it could cease to be the force it once was. Heterosexual couples will continue to exist but not principally for purposes of reproduction (for which other specific techniques exist). Couples will have the freedom to meet and form relationships in precisely the same way as homosexual couples do today—that is, for unadulterated pleasure. As far as procreation is concerned, ad hoc procedures would be freely available.

The above scenario understandably strikes fear into the hearts of sacred and secular conservatives who argue that our societies are undergoing a process of homosexualization where heterosexuals are imitating homosexual traits and practices and ignoring the vital links between sexuality and love on the one hand and between sexuality and procreation on the other. In essence, traditional thinking sees the sexual act as an upstream psychological predisposition (love) and a downstream physical ambition (reproduction), whereas male-female sexual relationships where genuine love and procreative intent are absent are today increasingly common. The conservative view is that this will have a debilitating effect on society. That view may well be justified, but the threat is not to society per se but to heterosexist society in all its monopolistic social and symbolic legitimacy. This may well spell *finis* to heterosexual culture as such, but it could also presage the advent of a new sexual and postsexual culture that still remains to be defined.

Conclusion

Several of my friends have at one time or another taken me to task for writing so frequently about homosexuality. Since I have been instrumental in setting up several not-for-profit associations in that sector and have produced two books and given numerous interviews on the subject, I take their point. At the same time, however, I have also been much occupied by French literary studies, devoting my dissertation to that area of interest and publishing four books and numerous articles in what has since emerged as my principal field of expertise. (To date, none of my friends has ever called into question my interest in *belles lettres*. One might perhaps ask what that says about them?) In any event, I have started writing progressively less about homosexuality, not least since my research provoked a *regressio ad principium* once my focus shifted from homosexuality to homophobia, from there to heterosexism, and, ultimately, to heterosexuality. Women's studies paved the way for men's studies, black studies for white studies. Similarly, researching gay and lesbian issues brought me full circle, paving the way for this study of heterosexuality.

In 1998, one of my friends introduced me to the young woman to whom he had recently become engaged. He explained to his wife-to-be that I was "into" gay and lesbian research. She immediately burst out laughing, clearly finding this unusual or even eccentric. She asked me if that was really what I spent my time doing and, when I replied in the affirmative, promptly burst into laughter again. Predictably, my friend was somewhat embarrassed by her reaction. The evening had started less than auspiciously, with none of us capable of extricating ourselves from an awkward situation (which she continued to find hilarious), and I decided I should take the bull by the horns.

"That's right," I said. "I've worked a lot on homosexual issues, and for the past few months, I've also been researching heterosexuality."

I thought she might find this even more amusing, and I composed myself for her reaction, expecting to be the butt of her laughter for days and weeks to come. She at once stopped laughing, however. She sounded upset. Her reply was curt:

"That's wrong! You mustn't do that! People will start to think there's something unnatural about heterosexuality."

She may have hit the nail on the head. That prompt and clear response convinced me she was far from being as empty-headed as she may initially have appeared. Besides, the brief exchange confirmed my determination to forge ahead, not least since she had insisted I should desist.

My research then stalled, held in abeyance by other pressing matters, among them an acrimonious debate on French civil partnership contracts and subsequent vicious and spiteful comments and articles that prompted me to begin compiling my *Dictionary of Homophobia*. It suddenly seemed important to start fighting on a much broader front. Accordingly, I organized the International Day against Homophobia and Transphobia (IDAHO), now celebrated in more than seventy countries, and took a proactive role in the launch of the Representative Council of Black Associations (CRAN), whose spokesman I remain to this day. Concurrently, I wrote a dissertation, held down a university post, and prepared a course of lectures for the University of Orléans.

As of 1998, I found myself unable to give my undivided attention to what was by then my favorite topic—heterosexual love. I published a number of articles on the subject in journals such as *Les Temps Modernes*, gave lectures on several occasions both in France and abroad, and even organized a postgraduate seminar within the framework of the Reims University DESS (Diplôme d'études supérieures spécialisées) Gender and Sexuality Programme, the brainchild of the late Gérard Ignasse. Sadly, however, I found I had next to no time to embark on in-depth research. To do justice to the subject matter, I estimated that at least four or even five years of research would be required. I was not in a position to earmark such a lengthy period for the project, and mounting commitments elsewhere made it increasingly unlikely I ever would be

In other words, it was perhaps for the best to let well enough alone and set my sights lower. The massive scope of such a project is such that there was no way to cover every aspect comprehensively. However, as La Fontaine famously pointed out, "loin d'épuiser une matière, il n'en faut prendre que la fleur" ("far from exhausting a subject, it suffices to skim off the cream"). It is fair to say that a full discussion of the themes touched on in these pages would run to several volumes.

This is the first book on the history of heterosexuality to be published in France, and as such, it admittedly has an agenda, the aim being to identify approaches rather than articulate conclusions. It may well be that one aspect or another could have been discussed at greater length, but the fact remains that such a vast subject cannot be covered in a single volume. I would add that my research has focused primarily on France and, by extension, on French-language documents and literature, both because this is the area with which I am personally most familiar and because literature has for a long time played such a key role in our national culture. It goes without saying that the present analysis needs to be complemented and, as and where necessary, adjusted to accommodate other forms of cultural expression and allow for disparate national and international perspectives.

As research into this sector intensifies, however, I am persuaded that, as is invariably the case, the *lacunae* and limitations of this pioneering study will be exposed. That is as it should be. Should others take over from where I have left off, so much the better: this book will have attained its prime objective—to open up a field of study.

It is appropriate to append here a word about methodology and approach. Since the term *heterosexuality* was not even in existence until the close of the nineteenth century, it may come as something of a surprise that it is applied in the course of research into premodern society. Is this not something of an anachronism? A valid question, perhaps, and certainly one that needs to be addressed.

At the risk of shocking the academic research community at large, however, I would reply only that all history is by definition anachronistic, inasmuch as the discipline looks backward (*ana*) in time (*chronos*), seeking to interpret past events and resolve issues that earlier generations were perhaps unable or unlikely to address. Investigating the causes of the French Revolution, for example, surely implies a more critical review of pre-1789 source materials than was open to contemporary commentators. What is vital is not to avoid the anachronistic (how can one?) but, instead, to remain alert to its implications.

Besides, one of the objectives of the present study is specifically to highlight the anachronistic nature of common perceptions. Any attempt to discuss the nature of love down through the ages is nugatory if one simply takes as one's point of departure the assumption that men have always loved women and praised their beauty. As John Boswell has rightly pointed out, that attitude was not always the norm—far from it. Such a smug assumption is typical of the complacent anthropologist who is overly anxious to postulate the universal from a study of the particular. Accordingly, it seemed appropriate to extend the scope of our analysis to examine the genealogy of heterosexuality in a bid to rehistoricize the anachronistic vision that is spontaneously—and culturally—ours.

It may be surprising to discover that the present "anachronistic" rewriting of history barely extends back beyond the medieval period. Strictly speaking, one should go back some way further, seeking the origins of heterosexual culture in classical antiquity and even earlier. The Hellenic period, for example, is worthy of investigation in that it spawned accounts of love and romance that, many centuries after the age of Pericles, presaged the heterosexual content of thirteenth-century (and also seventeenth-century) fiction. It is also instructive to explore classical mythology and Vedic tradition in a bid to put the man-woman duality into the overall context of Indo-European societies. This is an area of research to which I will return one day.

The archeological (essentially constructivist and diachronic) approach adopted here with regard to sexuality as a whole, has prompted some of my colleagues to invite me to clarify my position toward the late French philosopher, historian, and sociologist Michel Foucault. In response, I would say only that I have not sought to adopt any particular stance in this regard. Although we doubtless have some things in common, the principal difference between us (other than the quality and scope of his reflections) resides in the simple fact that Foucault authored a *History of Sexuality*, whereas I currently envisage a *History of Heterosexuality,* a study trilogy of which the present volume is only the first part. For me, moreover, the question is not so much "Why are we so preoccupied with sexuality?"—as Foucault asks up front in his *The Will to Knowledge*—but far rather, as the introduction to the present work inquires, "Why do we make so little mention of heterosexuality?" In essence, the "will to know" (sexuality) dissimulates a "will to conceal" (heterosexuality). If Foucault has a blind spot (and who among us has not at least one?), then it is in this respect. The first time I read his work, I concluded that, for him, heterosexuality was destined to remain essentially a dead letter.

It need scarcely be added that the present study adopts an essentially androcentric, or male-oriented, perspective. Other than the fact that I am myself male, two distinct reasons underpin my motives in this respect. On the one hand, what I have attempted to show is the development of heterosexual culture from within a social context where the female of the species was regarded exclusively as an object—to be celebrated, perhaps, but an object all the same. On the other hand, I have attempted to point up resistance to heterosexual culture, not least since, from the outset and for a long time, the culture of heterosexuality was also roundly criticized by the female of the species (cases in point being Christine de Pizan and, much later, George Sand). In a male-dominated society, however, criticisms articulated by women, however valid, were inevitably few and far between and, as such, carried no great weight. By contrast, disciples of the burgeoning women's movement of the twentieth century constituted a ready audience for critics such as the American feminist poet Adrienne Rich, the French theorist Monique Wittig, and the American philosopher Judith Butler. Accordingly, female attitudes to heterosexual culture, from the 1970s on, form an integral part of the present study.

Readers will also note that I have based my findings on official or so-called elite culture, and the present study takes little account of what we generally refer to as popular (pop) culture. The latter clearly merits study, but my immediate concern is to demonstrate how the present-day predominance of heterosexual culture can be traced to official institutions such as the Roman Catholic Church, the higher orders of the nobility, and, albeit to a lesser extent, the medical profession. Specifically, I have set out to illustrate official opposition to what was once perceived as an alternative culture but that was nonetheless destined to emerge as dominant in the longer term. That said, it would be most instructive to study heterosexual culture at the grassroots level, particularly in the current climate. One might investigate, for example, to what extent sports-related values are a modern reformulation of the chivalric ethos that celebrated *virtus* (variously *manliness, prowess, courage,* or *moral virtue*) and denounced *mollitia* (variously *softness, effeminacy,* or *sexual passivity*), while endorsing homosociality (nonsexual same-sex relationships) and excoriating homosexuality (a distinction the knights of the Middle Ages did not observe).

The extent to which the Christian ethic has yielded ground to secular republicanism also needs investigation. In France, for example, the black headgear of the *République* may have replaced the black cassock of the clergy, but the moral imperative remained in many ways unchanged, particularly as far as women were concerned. Thus, the "civilizing mission" proclaimed by the nineteenth-century French prime minister Jules Ferry was essentially an extension of Christian "missions" despatched to France's colonies.

One might also speculate on the extent to which the juxtaposition of homosociality against homosexuality is reflected in today's unwritten codes purporting to define masculine behavior and the extent to which those codes are based on a series of contradictory messages that push boys and young men toward homosociality (on condition they do not descend into homosexuality) and toward heterosexuality (provided they do not lapse into effeminacy). Is it not precisely this dichotomy that prompts many heterosexual males to find greater enjoyment in the company of male friends while at the same time exhibiting a sexual preference for women and that accounts for the fact that many homosexual males feel distinctly more at home in female company despite harboring a sexual preference for men? Investigating that issue may lie beyond the scope of the present study, but it is certainly something to be looked into at a future date.

We turn from methodology to tangible conclusions. A thousand years or so of heterosexual culture have elapsed since the dawn of the age of chivalry in Western society. This should not be taken to mean that heterosexuality appeared out of the blue as a twelfth-century invention, marking a break with the good old days when homosociality was the established and convenient norm. That would be plainly absurd and, moreover, wholly at variance with the contents of the present study, which postulates a shift in epistemological emphasis in acknowledgment of the fact that, while heterosexual practices might have been widespread, heterosexual cultures were not. To put it another way, the celebration of love between men and women was not a constant of premodern human society.

Available documentary evidence reveals that celebration of heterosexual love was a feature of eleventh-century Western society in the guise of courtly love. Its rapid spread was nothing short of remarkable, yet even more so was the resistance mounted by dominant interest groups such as the clergy and the nobility, the respective pillars of premodern society (or as Georges Dumézil has memorably labeled them, the *oratores* and the *bellatores*—those who pray and those who fight). In essence, the clergy opposed heterosexuality first and foremost on the straightforward grounds of its sexual nature, whereas their own ethos was rooted in renunciation of the pleasures of the flesh and a commitment to divine love. For its part, the nobility opposed heterosexuality principally on the grounds that it was precisely that (*hetero*), whereas their own ethos was predicated, as French medievalist Georges Duby has written, on virility, male bonding, and homosociality—same-sex relationships of a nonsexual nature. In a nutshell, one group deplored heterosexuality as an inevitable prelude to sexual debauchery, whereas the other group excoriated it as a symptom of weakness and effeminacy.

The clash between heterosexuality and the ethical position of the clergy and the nobility did not take the form of institutionalized opposition between two conflicting socially determined ideologies, each with its own designated spokesman and a clear sense of the issues at stake. As it happened, progress toward the legitimization of heterosexuality was slow rather than fluid, natural, and spontaneous. Along the way, it gave rise to serious differences of opinion, stubborn resistance, and even open conflict, yet it also engendered compromise, accommodation, and conciliation. The historical evolution described in these pages thus exhibits a particular dynamic sustained by the interplay of strong undercurrents that generate powerful shock waves whose effects became evident only over the long term.

Unable to hold back the floodtide of heterosexuality, the clergy and the nobility took stock and decided to assimilate what they could not reject. Accordingly, they tried to adapt and mold heterosexual culture to their own specific needs. More often than not, they were obliged to modify their traditional demands and expectations to accommodate this new and increasingly dominant culture. Whenever heterosexuality and its various manifestations were challenged or condemned as inimical to the chivalric code or religious doctrine, the aim was to project in its stead the notion of the noble warrior or the devout man of the cloth. Hero and saint were advanced as models for all to admire and emulate. In contrast, the new culture of heterosexuality seemed to vindicate (to the dismay of the nobility) effeminate courtiers rather than virile men of action and to sanction sinful sensual pleasure in place of the chastity advocated by an outraged clergy.

Confronted by the same situation, the modern medical profession opted for a decidedly more novel approach. First, it elected to endorse rather than challenge the norm of the heterosexual couple. As noted elsewhere, what little resistance the profession did offer was short-lived—not least since heterosexuality was already the norm by the time modern medicine came along. Second, the profession was prompt to accept the heterosexual as the norm and to set it off against the figure of the homosexual, who embodied perversion. Third, the "inverts" constructed by medical discourse were written off as effeminate and debauched—a criticism reminiscent of religious and chivalric objections to courtly behavior.

The overall position may be summarized in schematic form:

	Men of action	Clergy	Medical profession
Value +	Virtus	Chastity	Health
Relationships +	Homosocial	God/man	Man/woman
Model features +	Hero	Saint	Heterosexual
Value –	Mollitia	Fornication	Perversion
Relationships –	Heterosexual	Physical	Homosexual
Model features –	Effeminate	Debauched	Homosexual
Problem area	Gender	Sex	Sex and gender
Objection to heterosexual culture	Too hetero	Too sexual	None

Three points should be made with regard to the above schema. First, allowance must be made for the fact that it is synchronic as opposed to diachronic. Thus, the medical profession that substantially favored heterosexual relationships is the modern medical profession, and the church that strongly opposes all forms of physical love is the medieval church at the time of its peak authority and influence. (One should add that the modern church is doubtless more ready to admit expressions of physical love, just as the medical profession in ancient times was significantly less tolerant of heterosexual love.) Second, it is evident that both the positive and negative characteristics listed relate essentially to males. This should come as no great surprise, given that the medical profession, for example, expressed next to no interest in female-to-female sexuality. Further, when doctors did take an interest in anatomy, it was predominantly the male anatomy (other than when examination was specifically gynecological). Third and most significant, the contemporary codes of heterosexuality have been shaped by all three systems of thought.

However banal and obvious this term-by-term juxtaposition of *homo* (same) and *hetero* (different) appears today, the fact remains that it was actually less pertinent in the Middle Ages, when "sodomites" constituted no more of a distinct societal grouping counterbalanced by "nonsodomites" than "liars" were grouped as distinct from those who spoke the truth. Sodomy and mendacity were both considered sinful, however, and sinners were the diametrical opposite of saints. For all that, as Michel Foucault noted in *The Will to Knowledge*, the sodomite was not viewed as a particular category of individual and, as such, had no identified social opposite.

Despite how straightforward and commonplace it may appear today, the heterosexual/homosexual juxtaposition was actually less to the fore in premodern times and, in effect, was not universally observed. Equally, heterosexual love—however natural it may appear today—was seen in those earlier societies not so much as a rejection of homosexuality but rather as an alternative to nonsexual male-to-male relationships and, for that matter, the love of God advocated respectively by chivalric and religious practices and codes of conduct.

There is today a clear need to rethink our attitude to heterosexuality, which is, at one and the same time, celebrated and routinely dismissed as routine and an accepted fact of life. To my mind, heterosexuality does not deserve to be treated in this manner. As a subject, it is regrettably something of an orphan—neglected by academics and intellectuals and also largely ignored by society as a whole. In fact, heterosexuality is accepted as an automatic condition that many people spontaneously espouse and replicate on a daily basis as a component of middle-class values. It is for this reason that I believe nothing short of an epistemological breakthrough of Copernican proportions is indicated if heterosexuality is to reassert its own cultural identity.

The dimensions of the problem are such that it should be addressed by virtually everyone, including homosexuals. After all, heterosexuality is too important an issue to be left to heterosexuals alone. One might add that the topic of heterosexuality is one that, although rarely addressed, is capable of generating genuine and widespread interest: although little has been written on heterosexuality as a subject, it is part of the daily life of many people throughout the world.

Le Petit Robert—the lexicon that, together with its big brother *Le Grand Robert*, is an acknowledged authority on the French language—at one point defined *heterosexuality* as "normal sexual practice among heterosexuals," a *heterosexual* being elsewhere defined as "one who exhibits a normal sexual preference for those of the opposite sex." That, in itself, would have been enough to send any serious commentator on comparative values into what can only be described as some form of axiological orbit.

Le Petit Robert subsequently had second thoughts, and in a moment of (relative) lucidity, its compilers proposed the modified definitions that still appear in the 2008 edition—"Heterosexuality: heterosexual sexual preference (regarded as normal)" and "Heterosexual: one who exhibits a sexual attraction (considered normal) for individuals of the opposite sex." A small step for sexuality, certainly, but a giant leap for the *Petit Robert?* Not quite. As sociologist Éric Fassin has rightly pointed out, "heterosexuality is not normal, it is declared to be the norm." By contrast, the entries in the *Petit Robert* would appear to suggest that homosexuality is abnormal by defining it as the "opposite of normal."

The 2008 pocket edition of the *Robert* has thankfully taken matters at least one step further by eschewing any value judgment in its definition of *heterosexual* as "one who exhibits a sexual preference for those of the opposite sex," thus deleting any reference to *normal* and removing any connotations of normality or abnormality.

Isn't it high time *Le Petit Robert*—and society in general—followed suit?

Notes

Preface

1. See, for example, Bernard Sergent, *Homosexualité et initiation chez les peuples indo-européens* (Paris: Payot, 1996), which argues that the traditional practice of pederasty in ancient Greece is broadly representative of Indo-European society as a whole, the Greek example being merely the most amply documented.
2. See John J. Winkler, *The Constraints of Desire: The Anthropology of Sex and Gender in Ancient Greece* (New York: Routledge, 1990); K. J. Dover, *Greek Homosexuality* (Cambridge: Harvard University Press, 1978); David M. Halperin, *One Hundred Years of Homosexuality and Other Essays on Greek Love* (New York: Routledge, 1990).
3. From "Sea of Love," a popular American song recorded in 1959 by Phil Phillips.
4. From another popular song that also made the American hit parade, "The Game of Love," recorded by Wayne Fontana and the Mindbenders in 1965.
5. John Boswell, *Same-Sex Unions in Premodern Europe* (New York: Vintage, 1995), xix–xx.

Part I: Chivalric Opposition to Heterosexual Culture

1   The Middle Ages

1. This feature is common to virtually all societies—martial, rural, or otherwise—that are founded on the basis of separation of the sexes, whereby the cult of male bonding takes precedence over that of heterosexual love.

2. Georges Duby, *Women of the Twelfth Century*, vol. III, *Eve and the Church*, trans. Jean Birrell (Chicago: University of Chicago Press, 1998), 92.
3. Boswell, *Same-Sex Unions in Premodern Europe*, xix.
4. John W. Baldwin, *The Government of Philip Augustus: Foundations of French Royal Power in the Middle Ages* (Berkeley: University of California Press, 1986), 21.
5. *The Song of Roland*, 107, trans. Glyn Burgess (Harmondsworth: Penguin, 1990), 73.
6. Ibid., 127, 82.
7. Ibid., 148, 92.
8. Ibid., 149, 93.
9. *La Chanson de Roland*, ed. Guillaume Picot (Paris: Larousse, 1972).
10. Bertrand de Bar-sur-Aube, *Girart de Vienne* (Paris: Société des anciens textes français, 1977).
11. Anon., *Daurel et Beton* (Paris: Paul Meter, 1880).
12. Anon., *Li Romans d'Athis et Procelias*, ed. Marie-Madeleine Castellani (Paris: Champion, 2006).
13. Ibid., ll. 306–307.
14. Ibid., ll. 3002–3003 and 3006–3007.
15. Anon., *Ami et Amile*, ed. Peter F. Dembowski (Paris: Champion, 1987).
16. Anon., *Ami and Amile: A Medieval Tale of Friendship*, trans. Samuel N. Rosenberg and Samuel Danon (Ann Arbor: University of Michigan Press, 1996), 35–36.
17. Ibid., 130.
18. The term *matière de Bretagne* is used in respect to both medieval Britain and Brittany, as opposed, for example, to *matière antique* and *matière de France*.
19. Jacques Le Goff, *Medieval Civilization, 400–1500*, trans. Julia Barrow (Oxford: Blackwell, 1988), 351.
20. René Nelli, *L'Érotique des troubadours* (Toulouse, France: Privat, 1963), 286.
21. Denis de Rougemont, *Love in the Western World*, trans. Montgomery Belgion (Princeton: Princeton University Press, 1983).
22. Chrétien de Troyes, *Erec and Enide*, trans. Carleton W. Carroll, in *Arthurian Romances* (London: Penguin, 2004), 67.
23. Ibid., 68.
24. Chrétien de Troyes, *The Knight with the Lion (Yvain)*, trans. William W. Kibler, in *Arthurian Romances*, 327.
25. Ibid., 330.
26. It should be added that *Erec and Enide*, *The Knight with the Lion*, and various other contemporary and later works demonstrate that—although it is encountered predominantly in extraconjugal contexts—*courtoisie* was also of major concern to married couples.

27. Legend has it that young Tristan, an orphan at the court of his uncle, King Marc, slays the cruel giant Moholt but, wounded in the combat, puts ashore in Ireland, where he meets the fair Iseult whom he is due to escort to Marc, her husband-to-be. Instead, the pair inadvertently drink a love potion that stirs in them the guilty yet all-consuming passion that will prove central to their destiny.

28. Eilhart von Oberg, *Tristrant und Isalde*, ed. Danielle Buschinger (Berlin: Weidler, 2004).

29. Uncle/nephew relationships are a recurrent theme in chivalric literature. In *The Song of Roland*, for example, the term *love* is repeatedly used to describe Charlemagne's relationship with his nephew. This passionate avuncular relationship is also very much in evidence in the German epic poem *Waltharius* (Walter of Aquitaine), most notably in the case of Hagen and Patavrid. Georges Duby points out that such relationships played an important role in feudal society: "The arrangement of family relationships in knightly society attributed to the maternal uncle certain rights and duties with regard to his nephews. . . . The uncle expected his sister's sons to love him better than their own father, and he himself felt called on to love them more than the latter. Notably, to help them in their career. Now in most cases, this man was in a better position to do so, since by the effect of matrimonial strategies the wife was usually of higher birth than her husband. In order to make their way in the world, the boys consequently 'turned' in the direction of their maternal ancestry. When they had been dedicated to the service of God, they rose within the ecclesiastical ranks thanks to the uncle who was a canon, abbot, or bishop; when they were knights, they set out to do battle in the troops of the uncle who was a knight-banneret, certain of finding in his entourage a firm support, a warm friendship, and the most assured opportunities of making their fortune." Georges Duby, *William Marshal: The Flower of Chivalry*, trans. Richard Howard (New York: Pantheon Books, 1986), 76–77.

30. *Lancelot of the Lake*, trans. Corin Corley (Oxford: Oxford University Press, 2008).

31. Ibid., 291.

32. Ibid., 291–292.

33. Ibid., 292.

34. Ibid., 300.

35. Ibid., 307.

36. Ibid., 323.

37. Ibid., 324.

38. See John Boswell, *Christianity, Social Tolerance, and Homosexuality: Gay People in Western Europe from the Beginning of the Christian Era to the*

Fourteenth Century (Chicago: University of Chicago Press, 1980). Boswell hypothesizes the existence of a gay culture in medieval times. Although this may be open to debate, he is unquestionably right when he asserts that, in the West, condemnation of sodomy was not widespread until the thirteenth century.

39. *Lanval*, in *The Lais of Marie de France*, trans. Glyn Burgess and Keith Busby (London: Penguin, 1999), 76.

40. Quoted in William Burgwinkle, *Sodomy, Masculinity, and Law in Medieval Literature: France and England, 1050–1230* (Cambridge: Cambridge University Press, 2004), xi.

41. Ibid, xii.

42. Guillaume de Lorris and Jean de Meun, *The Romance of the Rose*, trans. Frances Horgan (Oxford: Oxford University Press, 2008), 67.

43. Andreas Capellanus, *The Art of Courtly Love*, trans. John Jay Parry (New York: Columbia University Press, 1990), 30.

44. Cf. a letter on the subject of the Templars of Beaucaire addressed to Philip IV by *commissaire* Odard de Molinier: "Should one brother wish to lie with another, then the latter shall consent and endure this with no show of repugnance, inasmuch as this is expressly permitted under the statutes and laws of their order." Quoted in César de Nostredame, *Histoire et chronique de Provence* (Lyon, France: S. Rigaud, 1614), 324.

45. Malcolm Barber, *The New Knighthood: A History of the Order of the Temple* (Cambridge: Cambridge University Press, 1994), 302.

46. Yannick Carré, *Le Baiser sur la bouche au Moyen Âge. Rites, symboles, mentalités à travers les textes et les images. xie–xve siècle.* (Paris: Le Léopard d'or, 1992).

2 The Renaissance

1. *Discours sur les courronels de l'infanterie de France*, in *Œuvres complètes*, vol. VI, ed. Ludovic Lalanne (Paris: Renouard, 1873), 28.

2. Laurent Avezou, "Henri III," in *The Dictionary of Homophobia: A Global History of Gay and Lesbian Experience*, ed. Louis-Georges Tin, trans. Marek Redburn with Alice Michaud and Kyle Mathers (Vancouver: Arsenal Pulp Press, 2008), 223.

3. Courtly literature was frequently parodied in the sixteenth century, most notably perhaps in *Don Quixote*, where the aging knight, deluded yet obsessed by false notions of chivalry gleaned from courtly literature, sets off in search of his lady, the celebrated Dulcinea del Toboso. Although it may be difficult to conceive of a hero more preoccupied by heterosexual culture than Don Quixote, the entire thrust of Cervantes's novel actually stems from the male duo of Quixote and his trusty squire, Sancho Panza, who, in many respects, may usefully be compared to Pantagruel and Panurge.

4. Nicolas Filleul, *Les Théâtres de Gaillon à la Reine*, ed. Eugène de Robillard de Beaurepaire (Rouen, France: Imprimerie Henry Boissel, 1873).

5. Marc-Antoine Muret, *La Tragédie de Julius Caesar*, ed. Pierre Blanchard (Thonon-les-Bains: Alidades, 1995).

6. Jacques Grévin, *Théâtre complet et poésies choisies*, ed. Lucien Pinvert (Paris: Garnier, 1922); *César*, ed. Ellen S. Ginsberg (Geneva: Droz, 1971); *César*, ed. Jeffrey Foster (Paris: Nizet, 1974).

7. Louis Des Masures, *La Tragédie à l'époque d'Henri II et de Charles IX*, vol. II, ed. Enea Balmas and Michel Dassonville (Florence/Paris: Leo S. Olschki/ PUF, 1993).

8. In full, Marcus Atilius Regulus.

9. See Myriam Yardeni, *La Conscience nationale en France pendant les guerres de Religion (1559–1598)* (Paris/Louvain: Publications de la Sorbonne/B. Nauwelaertz, 1971), and Colette Beaune, *Naissance de la nation France* (Paris: Gallimard, 1985).

10. See Ullrich Langer and Jan Miernowski, eds., *Anteros* (Orléans, France: Paradigme, 1994).

11. Louis Des Masures, *David triomphant*, in *Tragédies saintes* (Paris: E. Cornély, 1907), l. 81.

12. Ibid., l. 105.

13. There are countless examples of how frequently these and similar stereotypical images feature in Petrarchan poetry. See sonnet 71 in Du Bellay's *L'Olive*, as well as his celebrated poem "À une dame" and the collection *Jeux rustiques*. See also sonnets 29 and 127 in Olivier de Magny's *Les Soupirs*. In addition to these examples, one might cite the plethora of imitations of the *Romance of the Rose*.

14. Here is a list of some of the collections where the word *amour* appears directly in the title: *Amores* by Du Bellay; *Amours* by Rémy Belleau; *Amours* by Christofle de Beaujeu; *Amours* by Jean de Sponde; *Amours* by Clovis Hesteau de Nuysement; *Amours, Continuation des Amours*, and *Nouvelle Continuation des Amours* by Ronsard; *Amours de Méline* and *Amours de Francine* by Jean-Antoine Baïf; *Amours de Diane* by Isaac Habert; *Les Amours d'Aymée* by Pierre de Brach; *Les Amours de Théophile* and *L'Amour passionnée de Noémie* by Marc Papillon de Lasphrise; *Amours de Diane* and *Amours d'Hippolyte, Diverses Amours*, and *Dernières amours* by Philippe Desportes; *Déploration d'Amour* by Mellin de Saint-Gelais; *Débat de Folie et d'Amour* by Louise Labé; *Discours des Champs faëz, à l'honneur et exaltation de l'amour et des dames* by Claude de Taillemont; *Erreurs amoureuses* and *Continuation des erreurs amoureuses* by Pontus de Tyard; *Soupirs amoureux* by François Béroalde de Verville; *Château d'amours* by Pierre Gringore; and even *Amour des amours* by Jacques Peletier. Many other works on the theme of love do not have the

word *love* in their titles: for instance, *Délie* by Maurice Scève, *L'Olive* by Du Bellay, *L'Olympe* by Grévin, *Le Printemps* by Théodore d'Agrippa d'Aubigné, *Les Soupirs* by Olivier de Magny, *Sonnets, odes et mignardises à l'admirée* by Jacques Tahureau, and so on.

3   The Seventeenth Century

1. Pierre Corneille, "On the Purpose and the Parts of a Play," in *Sources of Dramatic Theory*, vol. I, *Plato to Congreve*, ed. Michael J. Sidnell (Cambridge: Cambridge University Press, 1991), 239–240.

Part II: Ecclesiastical Opposition to Heterosexual Culture

4   The Medieval Church versus the Heterosexual Couple

1. This was a recommended path toward salvation, cf. Luke 18:28–30: "And He said unto them, 'Verily I say unto you, there is no man that hath left house, or parents, or brethren, or wife, or children, for the sake of the kingdom of God, who shall not receive manifold more in this present time and in the world to come life everlasting.'" See also Matthew 19:27–30 and Mark 10:20–21. In the Gospel according to Saint John, friendship is often presented as the essence of *caritas*: "Greater love hath no man than this, that a man lay down his life for his friends." (All quotations are from the Authorized King James Version.)
2. 1 Corinthians 7:1–2 and 8–9.
3. Jacques Poumarède, "Célibat," in *Dictionnaire du Moyen Âge*, ed. Claude Gauvard, Alain de Libera, and Michel Zink (Paris: PUF, 2002). See also Nicole Grévy-Pons, *Célibat et Nature, une controverse médiévale* (Paris: CNRS, 1975).
4. Duby, *Women of the Twelfth Century*, 3–4.
5. Jacques Le Goff, *The Medieval Imagination*, trans. Arthur Goldhammer (Chicago: University of Chicago Press, 1988), 102.
6. Christiane Klapisch-Zuber, ed., *A History of Women in the West*, vol. II, *Silences of the Middle Ages* (Cambridge: Belknap Press of Harvard University Press, 1992), 20.
7. Although married to Sarah, Abraham—the progenitor of Christianity—has several concubines. This does not appear to pose a problem. Nor, for that matter, does King Solomon, the fount of wisdom and justice, who boasts a *harim* of no fewer than one thousand wives.
8. *Vie de saint Alexis*, ed. Maurizio Perugi (Geneva: Droz, 2000).
9. Capellanus, *The Art of Courtly Love*, 194–195.
10. Ibid., 201.
11. Ibid., 211.

12. See Matthew 25:1–3.

13. Capellanus, *The Art of Courtly Love*, 187.

14. Nelli, *L'Érotique des troubadours*, 67.

15. Matfre Ermengaud, *Le Breviari d'amor*, ed. Gabriel Azaïs (Geneva: Slatkine, 1977), ll. 27,341–27,348.

16. See Nelli, *L'Érotique des troubadours*, 266: "Celui-là fait des poésies déshonnêtes / Qui dit des choses laides et viles / Ou qui requiert quelque don / Non permis et non convenable / Ou qui à celle où l'amour l'arrête / Demande ce qui est déshonnête, / Comme un baiser ou quelque autre faveur / Qui donnerait occasion de pécher. / Car aussitôt l'amour défaut / Quand le péché vient l'assaillir."

17. Josiane Teyssot, "Le mariage, entrée de la femme dans l'espace privé au Moyen Âge," in *Regards croisés sur l'œuvre de Georges Duby. Femmes et féodalité*, ed. Annie Bleton-Ruget, Marcel Pacaut, and Michel Rubellin (Lyon, France: Presses universitaires de Lyon, 2000), 245.

18. Quoted in *Anthologie de la poésie française* (Paris: Gallimard, 2000), 172.

19. Ibid., 174.

20. See Nelli, *L'Érotique des troubadours*, 264.

21. "Chanson mariale anonyme," in *Recueil de chansons pieuses du XIIIᵉ siècle*, ed. Edward Järnström, *Annales academiae scientarum fennicae*, vol. IV (Helsinki: 1910), 26–28.

22. See Gérard Gros, *Le Poème du puy marial. Étude sur le serventois et le chant royal du XIVᵉ siècle à la Renaissance* (Paris: Klincksieck, 1996).

23. Quoted in Boswell, *Christianity, Social Tolerance, and Homosexuality*, 211.

24. Ibid., 277.

5 The Renaissance

1. Georges Dotti, "Introduction," in *Chansons spirituelles*, by Marguerite de Navarre (Geneva: Droz, 1971), x.

2. De Navarre, *Chansons spirituelles*, 38.

3. Gaston Paris, ed., *Chansons du XVᵉ siècle* (Paris: Didot, 1975), 50: "Trop penser m'y font amours,"

4. De Navarre, *Chansons spirituelles*, 54: "O l'espinette du bois Mon amour la désire."

5. Ibid., 78.

6. Quoted in *La Polémique protestante contre Ronsard*, vol. II (Paris: Didier, 1973), 233: "Ronsard et ses ronsins je laisse ronsarder. / Qu'avec ses Ronsardeaux il ronsarde et ronsine, / Hannisse apres Marie, et Cassandre, et Francine. / De tout son ronsarder qu'il tient de si grand pris, / Rien apprendre ne veux, et n'en ay rien appris / Ains tousjours ay eu soin et diligente cure / D'apprendre mieux ailleurs que d'un porc d'Epicure."

7. Ibid., 82: "Or comme tu ensuis, en tes vers impudiques, / L'ordre et l'invention des Poëtes antiques / Tu imites leurs meurs, et devenant pourceau, / T'efforces d'Epicure augmenter le trouppeau."

8. Ibid., 79: "De Beze en sa jeunesse aimant la Poësie / Se feignit amoureux, et cette fantasie / (Dont il n'est à louer) si fort l'ensorcela, / Que sa folie mesme en ses vers decela . . . / Quand Dieu bruslant son cœur d'une ardeur trop meilleure / D'un coup luy feit changer de stile et de demeure / Afin qu'apres David, il apprint aux François / Comm'il faut louer Dieu, et d'esprit et de voix."

9. Ibid., 86.

10. Quoted in Pierre Perdrizet, *Ronsard et la Réforme* (Geneva: Slatkine, 1970), 65.

11. Ibid., 68–69: "Comment! Y avois tu leu / Pour les mettre ainsy au feu, / Quelque parolle hereticque / De la secte luthericque? / Hé Dieu! Elle ne sentoit rien / rien moins que luthérien."

12. Gabrielle de Coignard, *Spiritual Sonnets: A Bilingual Edition*, ed. and trans. Melanie E. Gregg (Chicago: University of Chicago Press), 43.

13. See ibid., 159: "Ronsard is immortal on earth and in heaven. / We inherit here his precious labors. / Seeing God face to face, he possesses the sky."

14. Jean-Marie Mayeur, Charles Pietri, André Vauchez, and Marc Venard, eds., *Histoire du christianisme*, vol. VIII (Paris: Desclée de Brouwer, 1992), 1139.

15. John Calvin, *Institutes of the Christian Religion*, trans. Henry Beveridge (Peabody, MA: Hendrickson, 2007), 824.

16. "By faith alone, grace alone, scripture alone."

17. "The Girl with No Interest in Marriage," in *Erasmus on Women*, ed. Erika Rummel (Toronto: University of Toronto Press, 1996), 29.

18. Ibid., 31.

19. Sara F. Matthews Grieco, "The Body, Appearance, and Sexuality," in *A History of Women of the West*, vol. III, *Renaissance and Enlightenment Paradoxes*, ed. Natalie Zemon Davis and Arlette Farge (Cambridge: Belknap Press of Harvard University Press, 1992), 84.

20. Michel de Montaigne, "On Affectionate Relationships," in *The Complete Essays*, trans. M. A. Screech (London: Penguin, 2003), 212.

6 The Seventeenth Century

1. Jacques du Bosc, *L'Honneste femme* (Paris: Jeantiste Loyons, 1662).

2. "Sermon LXII contre les bals, les danses ou les comédies et autres divertissements mondains qui sont les allumettes de luxure," in *Le Missionnaire de l'oratoire ou sermon pour les avents, carêmes et fêtes de l'année*, vol. II (Toulouse, France: 1688), 467–491.

3. Quoted in *Literary Criticism: Plato to Dryden*, ed. Allan H. Gilbert (Detroit: Wayne State University Press, 1962), 598.

4. Quoted in Jean-Paul Desaive, "The Ambiguities of Literature," trans. Arthur Goldhammer, in *A History of Women of the West*, vol. III (Cambridge, MA: Belknap Press, 1993), 270.

5. Act 1, scene 1.

6. Act 2, scene 6.

7. Act 5, scene 3.

8. Bernard Le Bouyer de Fontenelle, *Vie de Corneille*, in *Œuvres*, vol. III (1742), 103.

7 The Twentieth Century

1. Matthew 19:6.

2. Henry Phillips (in collaboration with Aude Pichon and Louis-Georges Tin), *Le Théâtre catholique en France au XXe siècle* (Paris: Champion, 2007). The author gratefully acknowledges material drawn from this collaborative work with respect to twentieth-century Catholic theater.

3. *La Vie catholique* 373 (November 21, 1931): 21.

4. "Les œuvres . . .," *Correspondant* (1922), 370.

5. Ibid., 39, 66.

6. Ferdinand-Antonin Vuillermet, *Les Divertissements permis et les divertissements interdits* (Paris: Lethielleux, 1925), 159–162.

7. Ibid., 164–165.

8. See Martine Jey, *La Littérature au lycée* (Paris: Klincksieck, 1998), 137.

9. Quoted in www.academiefrancaise.fr/immortels/base/academiciens/fiche.asp?param=541.

10. *Archives historiques de l'Archevêché de Paris* (Archives of the Archbishopic of Paris), series 1D, 43.

11. *Mandements, lettres et instructions pastorales de son Éminence le Cardinal Dubois Archevêque de Paris* (Lent 1933).

12. *Bulletin trimestriel* (April 15, 1924), 10.

13. *Revue des Lectures* (April 15, 1931), 392.

14. Censorship was reinstated by the Vichy régime under the aegis of the Ministry of Information. See Serge Added, *Le Théâtre dans les années de Vichy* (Paris: Ramsay, 1992), 37.

15. Ibid., 9.

16. *Le Soir*, July 19, 1927.

17. *Le Soir*, March 6, 1926.

18. Phillips, *Le Théâtre catholique en France au XXe siècle*, 123.

19. Ibid.

20. Jean-Yves Le Naour, "La Première Guerre mondiale et la régénération du théâtre," *Revue d'histoire du théâtre* 211 (2001): 229.

Part III: Medical Opposition to Heterosexual Culture

8   Heterosexual Love and Medieval and Renaissance Medicine

1. Jacques Le Goff, *La Civilisation de l'Occident médiéval* (Paris: Flammarion, 1982), 187.
2. Ibid., 194.
3. Jean Aubéry, *L'Antidote d'amour: Avec un ample discours contenant la nature et les causes d'iceluy, ensemble les remèdes les plus singuliers pour se préserver et guérir des passions amoureuses* (Paris: Claude Chappelet, 1599).
4. The reference to Virgil and Alexis is amusing to the extent that Alexis was not a woman but a young man. Jean Aubéry may have deliberately heterosexualized this pairing, or he may simply have erred in his assumption that Alexis was female. Mistakes of this kind were common in medieval times. In his famous *Ballade des dames du temps jadis*, François Villon alludes to Alcibiades as the beautiful "lady" allegedly in love with Socrates in Plato's *Symposium*.
5. As it happens, Ronsard is the poet *par excellence* of spring or, to be more precise, of early spring. The word *April* appears with remarkable regularity in his work (in sonnets 14, 60, 89, 115, and 117 in his collection of *Amours* dating from 1552 to 1553). It was also in April that Ronsard first met his true love, Cassandra Salviati.
6. Jacques Ferrand, *De la maladie d'amour ou melancholie erotique. Discours curieux qui enseigne à cognoistre l'essence, les causes, les signes et les remèdes de ce mal fantastique* (1610) (Paris: Denis Moreau, 1622); *A Treatise on Lovesickness*, trans. Donald A. Beecher and Massimo Ciavolella (Syracuse: Syracuse University Press, 1990).
7. See, for example, Joachim Du Bellay, *The Regrets*, sonnet 91, trans. David R. Slavitt (Evanston: Northwestern University Press, 2004), 197: "O lovely hair, silver and in a stern / Chignon! O brow with corrugated creases! / O face of sunburned bronze with masterpieces / Of glass eyes! O large mouth with a downward turn! / What would Petrarch say of those teeth, black / As ebony—a precious wood, I think— / And that smile provoking laughter or just a wink? / And the damascene throat where one can trace the track / Of interesting textures! And huge hooters! / And the long fingernails on the short fingers that suitors / Must learn to admire. And those great piano legs, / Beneath a body beyond comparison . . . / (At any rate, I haven't thought of one / To earn that embrace for which the whole world begs)."
8. Jean Fernel, *La Pathologie* (Paris: Vve J. Le Bouc, 1646), 502.
9. At 90c.
10. See chapter 32.

10   The Twentieth Century: The Last Traces of Medical Opposition

1. André Breton, *Œuvres complètes*, vol. I (Paris: Bibliothèque de la Pléiade), 948.

2. A.-E. Portemer, "De l'érotomanie au point de vue médico-légal" (thesis submitted to the Faculté de médecine de Paris, 1902), 10.

3. Gaston Ferdière, "L'Érotomanie, illusion délirante d'être aimé" (dissertation submitted to the Faculté de médecine de Paris, 1937), 70.

4. Portemer, "De l'érotomanie au point de vue médico-légal," 65.

5. Ferdière, "L'Érotomanie," 70.

6. Ibid., 24.

7. Irène Marcianne Gluck, "À propos de deux cas de psychoses passionnelles. De l'érotomanie à la question de la féminité" (doctoral thesis submitted to Université Paris-V, 1973), 26.

8. Portemer, "De l'érotomanie au point de vue médico-légal," 34.

9. Jonathan Ned Katz, *The Invention of Heterosexuality* (Chicago: University of Chicago Press, 2007), 92.

10. Ibid., 84.

11. Ibid., 86.

12. Juliette Rennes, *Le Mérite et la Nature. Une controverse républicaine: l'accès des femmes aux professions de prestige (1880–1940)* (Paris: Fayard, 2007), 332.

13. Ibid., 358.

14. Sigmund Freud, *Three Essays on the Theory of Sexuality*, trans. James Strachey (New York: Basic Books, 2000), 12.

15. Sigmund Freud, "The Psychogenesis of a Case of Homosexuality in a Woman," in *The Standard Edition of the Complete Psychological Works of Sigmund Freud*, vol. XVIII, trans. James Strachey (London: Vintage, 2001), 151.

16. Pierre-Olivier de Busscher, "Psychiatry," in *The Dictionary of Homophobia*, 379.

17. Paradoxically, geneticists in the United States are nowadays concerned to legitimize homosexuality by isolating it on one branch or other of the X-chromosome. If they are successful, homosexuality could come to be accepted as natural in the context of U.S. society. To date, results are inconclusive.

18. De Busscher, "Treatment," in *The Dictionary of Homophobia*, 473.

19. This is the day the present author went on to propose as the International Day against Homophobia and Transphobia, now celebrated annually in more than seventy countries worldwide and accorded official recognition by the European Parliament and the governments of Belgium, the United Kingdom, Mexico, Costa Rica, France, Luxembourg, the Netherlands, Brazil, and other countries.

20. See, in particular, Simon LeVay, *Queer Science: The Use and Abuse of Research into Homosexuality* (Cambridge: MIT Press, 1996), and Vernon A. Rosario, ed., *Science and Homosexualities* (New York: Routledge, 1997).

21. De Busscher, "Ex-Gay," in *The Dictionary of Homophobia*, 169–170.

22. It might be argued that, if one could establish why some people tend to be homosexual, one might also be able to establish why others tend to be heterosexual. To put it another way, the illusory "homosexual brain" might reveal by inference the secrets of the "heterosexual brain." To date, the existence of neither has been demonstrated or scientifically defined. That being so, one is tempted to conclude that heterosexuality—like homosexuality—must remain as yet a largely unexplained phenomenon.

23. A. S. Neill, *Summerhill: A Radical Approach to Child Rearing* (Harmondsworth: Penguin, 1961), 207.

24. Pierre Albertini, "School," in *The Dictionary of Homophobia*, 408.

25. Ibid., 408–409.

26. Ibid., 409.

27. It may be argued with some justification that the feminist movement (rightly or wrongly) identified coeducation as a means of promoting sexual equality. This was not, however, the initial aim. It is worth recalling that the benefits of mixed schooling are also mixed inasmuch as girls sometimes appear to underperform, and teachers may at times exhibit a tendency to overstate boys' achievements. Overall, it may be that coeducation is less beneficial in the case of young girls, but this need not imply that it should be scrapped. But since it was brought in without due consideration having been given to the sexual equality it purported to represent, it should come as no surprise that its effects have not been those it was never intended to achieve. To achieve equality, more was needed than simply introducing coeducation. In other words, the whole concept of coeducation should today be rethought rather than rejected outright.

28. See Rennes, *Le Mérite et la Nature*, 33.

29. The primacy of medical over religious opinion was particularly evident in France during the so-called *bataille du PACS*, when the Assemblée Nationale debated the desirability of formally acknowledging *Pactes Civiles de Solidarité*, civil society partnerships or civil marriages. In defense of the Vatican's position, Christine Boutin repeatedly attempted to mask her Catholic convictions behind a dense veil of pseudo-scientific rhetoric. Tony Anatrella, meanwhile, spoke against civil marriages as if from the point of view of psychiatry, neglecting to mention in newspaper reports that he was also a Catholic clergyman. The fact was that medical opinion was poised—one way or another—to carry the day and Catholic commentators perceived greater advantage in aligning themselves with "scientific opinion" than in advancing

theological arguments—not least in a country where church and state are separate.

30. André Gide, *Corydon*, trans. Richard Howard (Urbana: University of Illinois Press, 2001), 28–29.
31. Kate Millett, *Sexual Politics* (Urbana: University of Illinois Press, 2000), 275.
32. Ibid., 333.
33. Gayle Rubin, "The Traffic in Women: Notes on the 'Political Economy' of Sex," in *Toward an Anthropology of Women*, ed. Rayna R. Reiter (New York: Monthly Review Press, 1975).
34. Monique Wittig, *The Straight Mind and Other Essays* (Boston: Beacon Press, 1992), 35.
35. Judith Butler, "Imitation and Gender Insubordination," in *Inside/Out: Lesbian Theories, Gay Theories*, ed. Diana Fuss (New York: Routledge, 1991), 22.
36. The corollary would seem to be that homosexual practices are bad since they do not produce offspring. This assumes that homosexuals or bisexuals must be either sterile or oblivious to their moral duty to breed (an obligation even Catholic orthodoxy would reject, inasmuch as renouncing the pleasures of the flesh is considered the supreme virtue). Homosexual culture is also perceived as a danger because it is alleged to propagate sterility (while at the same time there is a refusal to recognize both the right to insemination in the case of lesbian couples and the existence of thousands of *de facto* homoparental families). Such is the paradoxical logic that underpins today's society.

Select Bibliography

Although there is a comparative dearth of material on heterosexuality, a bibliography based on terms such as *love* and *sexuality* would be so vast as to be unhelpful. Accordingly, the following truncated list of titles represents no more than a platform for further reflection.

Allen, Peter Lewis. *The Wages of Sin: Sex and Disease, Past and Present*. Chicago: University of Chicago Press, 2000.

Angeli, Giovanna, and Luciano Formisano, eds. *L'Imaginaire courtois et son double*. Naples: Edizioni Scientifiche Italiane, 1992.

Badinter, Élisabeth. *XY: On Masculine Identity*. Trans. Lydia Davis. New York: Columbia University Press, 1995.

Beattie Jung, Patricia, and Ralph F. Smith. *Heterosexism: An Ethical Challenge*. Albany: State University of New York Press, 1993.

Boswell, John. *Christianity, Social Tolerance, and Homosexuality: Gay People in Western Europe from the Beginning of the Christian Era to the Fourteenth Century*. Chicago: University of Chicago Press, 1980.

Brown, Peter. *The Body and Society: Men, Women, and Sexual Renunciation in Early Christianity*. New York: Columbia University Press, 2008.

Buschinger, Danielle, ed. *Amitié épique et chevaleresque*. Amiens: Presses du Centre d'études médiévales, 2002.

Butler, Judith. Imitation and Gender Insubordination. In *Inside/Out: Lesbian Theories, Gay Theories*, ed. Diana Fuss. New York: Routledge, 1991.

Capellanus, Andreas. *The Art of Courtly Love*. Trans. John Jay Parry. New York: Columbia University Press, 1990.

Carré, Yannick. *Le Baiser sur la bouche au Moyen Âge. Rites, symboles, mentalités à travers les textes et les images. XIe-XVe siècle*. Paris: Le Léopard d'or, 1992.

Ciavollela, Massimo. *La Malattia d'amore, dall'Antichita al Medioevo*. Rome: Bulzoni, 1976.

Damian, Peter. *Saint. Book of Gomorrah: An Eleventh-Century Treatise against Clerical Homosexual Practices*. Trans. Pierre J. Payer. Waterloo, ON, Canada: Wilfrid Laurier University Press, 1982.

Demurger, Alain. *Jacques de Molay. Le crépuscule des Templiers*. Paris: Payot, 2007.

de Rougemont, Denis. *Love in the Western World*. Trans. Montgomery Belgion. Princeton: Princeton University Press, 1983.

Duby, Georges. *Love and Marriage in the Middle Ages*. Trans. Jane Dunnett. Chicago: University of Chicago Press, 1994.

Duby, Georges. *William Marshal: The Flower of Chivalry*. Trans. Richard Howard. New York: Pantheon Books, 1986.

Duby, Georges, and Michelle Perrot, eds. *A History of Women in the West*. Cambridge: Belknap Press of Harvard University Press, 1992–1994.

Dufournet, Jean, ed. *Ami et Amile, une chanson de geste de l'amitié*. Paris: Champion, 1987.

Dumeige, Gervais, ed. *Histoire des conciles œcuméniques*. Paris: Éditions de l'Orante, 1982.

Duval, Sylvie. À propos de la notion d'érotomanie. Doctoral thesis submitted to Université de Caen, 1978.

Ferdière, Gaston. L'Érotomanie, illusion délirante d'être aimé. Thesis submitted to the Faculté de médecine de Paris, 1937.

Ford, Clellan S., and Frank A. Beach. *Patterns of Sexual Behavior*. Westport, CT: Greenwood Press, 1980.

Foucault, Michel. *The Will to Knowledge*. Trans. Robert Hurley. London: Penguin Books, 1998.

Gally, Michèle. *L'Intelligence de l'amour. D'Ovide à Dante. Arts d'aimer et poésie au Moyen Âge*. Paris: CNRS, 2005.

Gauvard, Claude, Alain de Libera, and Michel Zink, eds. *Dictionnaire du Moyen Âge*. Paris: PUF, 2002.

Gluck, Irène Marcianne. À propos de deux cas de psychoses passionnelles. De l'érotomanie à la question de la féminité. Doctoral thesis submitted to Université Paris-V, 1973.

Grévy-Pons, Nicole. *Célibat et Nature, une controverse médiévale*. Paris: CNRS, 1975.

Gros, Gérard. *Le Poème du puy marial. Étude sur le serventois et le chant royal du XIVe siècle à la Renaissance*. Paris: Klincksieck, 1974.

Katz, Jonathan Ned. *The Invention of Heterosexuality*. Chicago: University of Chicago Press, 2007.

Langer, Ullrich, and Jan Miernowski, eds. *Anteros*. Orléans: Paradigme, 1994.

Laqueur, Thomas. *Making Sex: Body and Gender from the Greeks to Freud*. Cambridge: Harvard University Press, 1990.

Leclerq, Jean. *Saint Pierre Damien, ermite et homme d'Église*. Rome: Edizioni di storia e letteratura, 1960.

Le Goff, Jacques. *Medieval Civilization, 400–1500*. Trans. Julia Barrow. Oxford: Blackwell, 1988.

Mayeur, Jean-Marie, Charles Pietri, André Vauchez, and Marc Venard, eds. *Histoire du christianisme*. Paris: Desclée de Brouwer, 1992.

Money, John. *Love and Love Sickness: The Science of Sex, Gender Difference, and Pair-Bonding*. Baltimore: Johns Hopkins University Press, 1980.

Nelli, René. *L'Érotique des troubadours*. Toulouse: Privat, 1974.

Perdrizet, Pierre. *Ronsard et la Réforme*. Geneva: Slatkine, 1970.

Pernoud, Régine. *Les Templiers*. Paris: PUF, 1974.

Phillips, Henry. *The Theatre and Its Critics in Seventeenth-Century France*. Oxford: Oxford University Press, 1980.

Phillips, Henry, Aude Pichon, and Louis-Georges Tin. *Le Théâtre catholique en France au XXe siècle*. Paris: Champion, 2007.

Pinaud, Jacques. *La Polémique protestante contre Ronsard*. Paris: Didier/STFM, 1973.

Portemer, A.-E. De l'érotomanie au point de vue médico-légal. Dissertation submitted to the Faculté de médecine de Paris, 1902.

Rennes, Juliette. *Le Mérite et la Nature. Une controverse républicaine: l'accès des femmes aux professions de prestige (1880–1940)*. Paris: Fayard, 2007.

Rich, Adrienne. Compulsory Heterosexuality and Lesbian Existence. *Signs* 5.4 (1980).

Telle, Émile V. *Érasme et le septième sacrement*. Geneva: Droz, 1954.

Tierney, Brian. *The Crisis of Church and State 1050–1300*. Toronto: University of Toronto Press, 1988.

Tin, Louis-Georges, ed. *The Dictionary of Homophobia: A Global History of Gay and Lesbian Experience*. Trans. Marek Redburn with Alice Michaud and Kyle Mathers. Vancouver, BC: Arsenal Pulp Press, 2008.

Wittig, Monique. *The Straight Mind and Other Essays*. Boston: Beacon Press, 1992.

About the Author

Louis-Georges Tin studied at the École normale supérieure and now lectures in the arts faculty of the University of Orléans and in the École des hautes études en sciences sociales (EHESS) of Paris, specializing in French literature and the history of sexuality. His publications include an anthology of sixteenth-century French poetry (Gallimard, 2005) and *Dictionary of Homophobia* (Arsenal Pulp Press, 2008). He is the founder of the Paris-based IDAHO Committee, which coordinates the International Day against Homophobia and Transphobia (May 17) celebrated each year in over one hundred associated countries worldwide, and is a cofounder of and chairperson for the Representative Council of Black Associations (CRAN). He is the recipient of several international awards in recognition of his contributions to human rights.

Index